Her Mast

in

Wharfedale

The Memorial Cross , Buckden Pike and 'Her'

Her Master's Walks in Wharfedale

Stephen I. Robinson

BARLEY · PUBLISHING
1998

Barley Publishing
10 Mill Green View
Swarcliffe
Leeds LS14 5JT

www.hm-walks.demon.co.uk
email: srobinson@hm-walks.demon.co.uk

ISBN 1 898550 02 6

Printed in Great Britain by:
Impressions (Leeds) Limited
The Mint, Moor View, Leeds LS11 9NF
Telephone 0113 246 1075

Upper Littondale from the Monk's Road

Contents

Paw-word by 'Her'

I will never forget my first visit to Wharfedale, it was to climb the massive mountain of Buckden Pike. When you're only sixteen inches tall everything does seem to be much larger.

The track was very muddy, but I managed to keep myself reasonably clean; he carried me over the worst areas *(the fool)*. At the top it was he who needed a rest, not me, but there again he had all the food, so I waited, to make sure I got my *rightful* share.

When we reached the memorial he said, "Look Sherry, a fox." *(Where? All I could see was a metal head)*. On the descent I wanted to get a move on, but he kept saying, "Steady on Little Un - ooh!!" One time, when I looked back he was lying flat on his back in the mud. *(Very strange behaviour if you ask me)*. He stopped in Starbotton to have a drink of a mucky brown liquid at the

Fox and Hounds. Once again the fox was in hiding *(very wise)*, but I did meet a very handsome labrador called Ben. Ben was going the same way as us, and so we walked together through the meadows back to Buckden.

I enjoy walking in the countryside, everyone seems to be much more courteous and friendly. They will pass the time of day and hold gates open for you. Amazing what fresh air can do *(or perhaps its that mucky brown liquid)*.

Some people we meet during our walks refer to me as a *nice* Jack Russell. JACK RUSSELL !*@#*! ME??? I may be nice - but I'm NOT a Jack Russell!!! I'm a SMOOTH FOX TERRIER, right?

Introduction

Wharfedale is probably the best known of the Yorkshire Dales and certainly one of the loveliest. Its breathtaking scenery and rich variety of flora and fauna put it in a class of its own.

The dale is named after its river, the Wharfe, which rises on Cam Fell, although it is known as Oughtershaw Beck until it reaches Beckermonds and merges with Greenfield Beck. The Wharfe is a well known angling river, but a difficult one to fish because of the exceptional clarity of the water. It retains this clarity as it plunges down narrow gorges and winds peacefully through lush meadows and woodland along the fertile valley floor. Only the heaviest of storms can taint the river slightly with the brown of the peat.

Wharfedale has some exceptionally beautiful villages each having its own distinctive charm. Large car parks at Buckden, Burnsall, Grassington and Kettlewell have made them popular centres for tourism. Hubberholme was a favourite haunt of J. B Priestley, the playwright. He venerated it as "the most peaceful spot on earth." Charles Kingsley was a frequent visitor to Arncliffe in Littondale where he wrote his famous novel *The Water Babies*. Turner, the artist, visited Wharfedale in 1816 making sketches for his grand *Histories of Yorkshire and Durham*.

The natural features of the Yorkshire Dales were formed over millions of years. The last major changes took place 10,000 years ago, at the end of the last Ice Age. Glaciers have covered much of Britain many times during the last two million years. They scoured the valleys of the dales and carved the characteristic U-shaped troughs with wide flat floors and steep sides. As the climate began to warm up the glaciers retreated, leaving behind lakes such as Malham Tarn and Semer Water. Further erosion, by rivers and streams, cut deep gorges, caves and potholes. Wind and rain played their part by weathering the limestone scars and pavements.

Man has also made his impact on the unique dales landscape. In AD 43, the Romans arrived and introduced a network of roads to make the area more accessible. Norse invaders of the ninth and tenth centuries cleared woodland and cultivated the upper dales. During the eleventh century the Normans built castles and established hunting forests.

One of the greatest influences on land usage was the monks. They developed superior farming and sheep breeding methods. Although wool was a source of great wealth, sheep farming had a severe effect on the landscape. Grazing prevented the growth of new trees which resulted in large areas of treeless grassland when the older trees died off.

The Yorkshire Dales provide some of the best opportunities for outdoor recreation, including angling, caving, climbing, horseriding and walking. These pastimes can, in their turn, have an adverse effect on the environment, litter, footpath erosion and traffic congestion being the most obvious. We should all take steps to minimise the effect that our activities may have on this sensitive environment. Our enjoyment of the countryside today must not be allowed to put at risk the enjoyment of others tomorrow.

Stephen I. Robinson,
June 1998

Be Prepared!

Walking, arguably the most enjoyable of pastimes and undoubtedly one of the healthiest, can be tailored to meet the requirements of almost anyone.

Your preference might be for a gentle stroll of three to four miles along a quiet riverbank or woodland path, or perhaps a strenuous hill walk of ten miles or more. Whichever you choose, provided you are properly equipped, your walk will not only be safer but also more enjoyable. This does not mean taking everything including the kitchen sink! If you are a keen photographer a camera with spare films is essential. Binoculars are mandatory for birdwatchers. The artist needs his sketchbook and pencil. But remember, everything you take is extra weight to be carried.

What to wear and carry will depend on the season, the weather and good sense. The items in the following lists are recommended, but think carefully about what to take. Some extra items may be needed on a hill walk which could be left behind when walking through the lower meadows. Due to our unpredictable climate, however, a spare wool sweater and waterproofs should always be carried. *(Items in italics could be used in warmer conditions.)*

TO WEAR

Strong walking boots or stout shoes
Thick woollen socks (two pairs)
Cotton shirt *or T-Shirt*
Walking breeches, trousers *or shorts* (Never wear jeans, they lose their heat retention when wet.)
Woollen hat, balaclava *or sun hat*

TO CARRY

A small rucksack about thirty litres capacity to carry the following:
Waterproof anorak or cagoule
Wool sweater or fibre pile jacket
Gloves, scarf
First aid kit, compass, whistle
Torch, pencil and notepad
Ordnance Survey map of area
Emergency rations, survival bag
Water bottle with water
Food and snacks

OPTIONAL ITEMS

Camera and spare films, binoculars
Swiss army knife
Flask with tea, coffee, soup or other hot drink
Waterproof overtrousers, gaiters
Five to ten metres of thin cord (Useful for temporary laces etc.)

Langstrothdale looking towards snowcapped Bucken Pike

About the Walks

This selection of walks explores the beautiful riverside scenery, high fells and limestone scars of Wharfedale. The variety of flora and fauna is outstanding and the villages are rich in character and diversity.

All of the walks follow circular routes ranging from 5¼ to 11¼ miles. They start from a car park where possible, or at a place where it is possible to park safely without inconveniencing others.

Final surveys were made between February and March 1998 and the maps amended accordingly. However, from time to time walls, fences and hedges may be removed, stiles and gates resited, buildings demolished and new plantations established. For this reason it is recommended that the relevant ordnance survey maps and a compass are carried. They will help to determine landmarks and alternative routes where necessary.

Only the relevant area of the map has been used and then simplified so that only the walls, fences, buildings, rivers, roads and landmarks etc. where the route passes are included.

Each map has the route marked in red with numbered arrow pointers relating to a descriptive guide on the facing page. This should help to avoid confusion, but common sense and some map reading experience is desirable.

The times given for completion of the walks are approximate and do not include any allowance for lunch breaks, photo stops or sightseeing. As a rule of thumb, adding one third of the stated time for stops should be sufficient. If accompanied by young children extra walking time will have to be allowed. Extended stays at any of the inns or tea shops *en route* should also be added to the time.

TROLLER'S GILL and KAIL HILL

from Barden Bridge (9 miles)

This is an easy walk beginning with a pleasant stroll along the Dales Way footpath. The river scenery is spectacular and panoramic views unfold throughout.

Barden Bridge, with its three high arches and angled buttresses, is a very elegant and impressive structure. The bridge was rebuilt in 1676 after being washed away in the disastrous flood of 1673. Bridges at Kettlewell, Burnsall, Bolton, Ilkley and Otley were also destroyed in the same flood.

Barden Tower, sited on the main road above the bridge, was built in the eleventh century as a hunting lodge in the Forest of Barden. It was rebuilt and the keep enlarged in 1485. The ruined but imposing shell of the tower remains. There is a chapel next to it and traces of an outer curtain wall and gate.

During most of its 900 year history the tower was owned by the Clifford Family who held title to the Honour of Skipton. In 1461, their estates were seized by Edward IV after the ninth Lord, 'Butcher' Clifford, was killed at the Battle of Towton. On the accession of Henry VII, in 1485, the estates were restored to Henry Clifford.

Henry was known as the 'Shepherd Lord.' Lady Clifford, fearing that the Yorkists might harm her son, had sent him to be raised secretly by a shepherd at Threlkeld near Keswick. In 1513, at the age of sixty, Henry led an army from local villages to help defeat James IV of Scotland at Flodden Field.

From Barden a pleasant riverside path is followed to Howgill Bridge and after a short climb to Howgill Lane there are extensive views of the dale. The route continues through the meadows to the peaceful hamlet of Skyreholme and on to Parcevall Hall.

Parcevall Hall stands in sixteen acres of exquisitely landscaped gardens with terraces, woodlands and nurseries. It is stocked with many rare plants and shrubs. The gardens are open to the public from Easter to October. Early records suggest that it was first called Parson's Hall, which is appropriate today because the Hall is now used as a retreat for the Diocese of Bradford.

The path to Troller's Gill passes the former Skyreholme Dam. The dam, which supplied water for a paper mill in the village, burst in 1899 and was never repaired. The mill is said to have had the largest waterwheel in the North of England.

Troller's Gill is a narrow, steep-sided limestone ravine about 300 yards long and just a few yards wide. The gill is usually dry but, after heavy rain, it can become a raging torrent. According to local folklore a barguest, the 'Spectre Hound of Craven,' lives in a cave near the gill. A cobbler from Thorpe, who had lost his way, saw the barguest and described it as, "Yellow, wi such eyes! they war as big as saucers. This mun be a barguest, thowt I, an' counted mesel for dead!" He escaped by crossing the beck. A barguest cannot cross running water!

After visiting the gill, the path leads to the remains of the Gill Head Mine. The mine closed long ago, but it was reworked for fluorite in the 1970's by a group of local men. The fluorite was concentrated in one large deposit at the side of the old lead vein.

During the descent to Woodhouse there are excellent views of Simon's Seat, Barden Moor, Thorpe Fell and the deep valley of Barben Beck. The dome shaped hill in the foreground is Kail Hill which is a good example of a reef knoll. Reef knolls are composed of pure limestone, rich in coral fossils and were formed 330 million years ago. An Iron Age camp existed on the summit of Kail Hill and a grinding stone was found near the site.

From Woodhouse a riverside path is followed back to Barden, allowing more of the River Wharfe's scenery and wildlife to be enjoyed.

Start/Parking:	Barden Bridge, the small car park by the riverside or in the car park belonging to the Bolton Abbey estate.
Location:	Barden Bridge is situated between Bolton Abbey and Burnsall, 6 miles north east of Skipton. Leave the B6160 at Barden Tower, signposted Appletreewick.
Grid Ref:	052 574.
Distance:	9 miles circular. Allow 4½ hrs.
OS Maps:	Outdoor Leisure Map 10 (1:25,000) or Landranger 104 and 98 (1:50,000).
Refreshments:	Cafés at Howgill Lodge and Barden Tower.
Public Toilets:	None.
Other:	None.

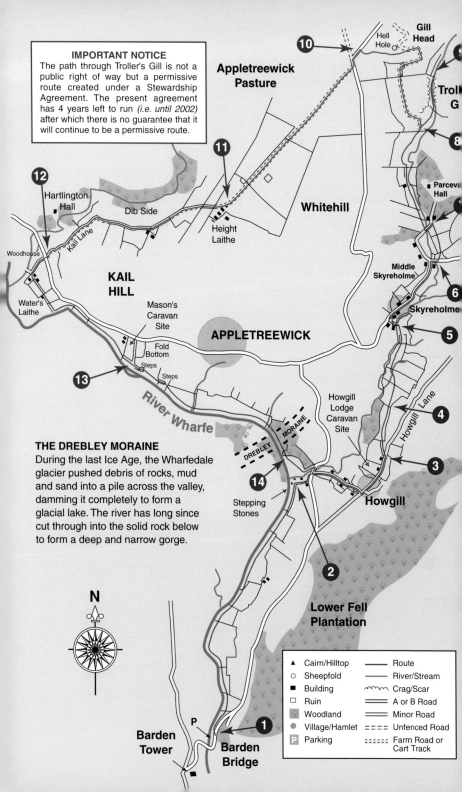

IMPORTANT NOTICE
The path through Troller's Gill is not a public right of way but a permissive route created under a Stewardship Agreement. The present agreement has 4 years left to run *(i.e. until 2002)* after which there is no guarantee that it will continue to be a permissive route.

Gill Head

Hell Hole

10

Appletreewick Pasture

Troll G

8

11

Parceva Hall

Hartlington Hall

12

Dib Side

Whitehill

Height Laithe

Kail Lane

Woodhouse

Middle Skyreholme

KAIL HILL

Water's Laithe

6

Skyreholme

5

Mason's Caravan Site

APPLETREEWICK

Fold Bottom

Steps

Steps

13

4

Howgill Lodge Caravan Site

Howgill Lane

River Wharfe

THE DREBLEY MORAINE
During the last Ice Age, the Wharfedale glacier pushed debris of rocks, mud and sand into a pile across the valley, damming it completely to form a glacial lake. The river has long since cut through into the solid rock below to form a deep and narrow gorge.

MORAINE

DREBLEY

14

3

Howgill

Stepping Stones

2

N

Lower Fell Plantation

P

Barden Tower

Barden Bridge

1

Symbol	Legend	Symbol	Legend
▲	Cairn/Hilltop		Route
○	Sheepfold		River/Stream
■	Building	⌒⌒⌒	Crag/Scar
□	Ruin		A or B Road
	Woodland		Minor Road
●	Village/Hamlet	= = = =	Unfenced Road
P	Parking	⋯⋯⋯	Farm Road or Cart Track

1 Troller's Gill and Kail Hill

1 *(GR 052 574)* Follow a narrow path behind the wall along the riverside. Bear left at a signpost *(SP Howgill 1m)* and go through a gate. Continue on a clear path staying close to the riverside and passing through several meadows.

2 *(GR 059 592)* Turn right at some huts. *(At the last survey there was also a green caravan at this point).* Turn left at a barn onto a good track which leads to the main road near Howgill Bridge. Cross the road and follow a walled track to Howgill Lane *(SP Howgill Lane).* Turn left and continue along the lane passing Howgill Lodge Caravan Site.

3 *(GR 065 594)* Leave the lane via a gate on the left *(SP Skyreholme).* Stay with the left wall through a gap stile and then follow the right wall through a gateway.

4 *(GR 065 597)* Bear left and descend to cross a ladder stile. Continue down to cross a small beck over a plank bridge. Turn right and go through a broken wall *(SP Skyreholme).* Follow the beck upstream to a wooden footbridge.

5 *(GR 066 603)* Cross the footbridge and climb some steps, bear right and continue to the road at Skyreholme. Turn right and follow the road to the junction near the telephone box. Turn right and cross the bridge over Skyreholme beck.

6 *(GR 069 607)* After a few yards leave the road over a stile *(SP Parcevall Hall).* Climb to the top right of the field and go through a gateway. Follow a clear path through two fields and over a stone step stile to join a farm lane.

7 *(GR 069 610)* Turn left and follow the lane. After crossing a wooden bridge go through a gate on the right *(SP Gill Head/New Road).* Continue on a clear path close to the beck through two gates and over a ladder stile. Bear left along a clear path above the former Skyreholme dam and cross a wooden stile.

8 *(GR 068 616)* *To visit Troller's Gill* bear right, the path becomes clearer as it reaches the beck side. Continue over a stile to the entrance of Troller's Gill, the path climbs gently through the gorge to a ladder stile at the top.

9 *(GR 069 620)* Retrace steps to point 8 and follow a path to the right *(SP footpath).* Continue along a clear track climbing over two wooden step stiles. At a sharp right bend leave the track going straight ahead, passing Hell Hole. Stay on this path and climb up to cross a ladder stile leading onto the main road.

10 *(GR 063 622)* Turn Left and follow the road round a left bend, after about 120 yards leave the road through a gate on the right *(SP Hartlington).* Continue on a good farm road via two gates to a fork.

11 *(GR 054 611)* Take the right fork and continue through a gate *(SP Bridleway).* Continue on an enclosed track through another gate *(SP Hartlington).* Stay on this track descending gently via three more gates to the main road.

12 *(GR 041 608)* Cross the road and go down the lane opposite *(SP Dales Way Path).* At the farm turn left *(SP Appletreewick)* and continue through three gates to reach the river at a bend. Stay close to the river over a stile and through two gates to Fold Bottom.

13 *(GR 047 600)* Bear left *(SP Howgill)* go over a stile, climb some steps and through a gate *(SP Footpath).* Continue downstream, go through another gate, climb some more steps, continue through two gates and then descend, returning to the riverside.

14 *(GR 058 594)* After passing through a wood, bear left and go through a gate which leads to the main road near Howgill Bridge. Turn right and cross the bridge. Leave the road at the first track on the right *(SP Barden Bridge 1m).* Return to Barden via the outward route.

BURNSALL, THORPE and LINTON

from Burnsall (7½ miles)

Three of Wharfedale's villages are visited during this leisurely walk; Burnsall with its beautiful riverside setting, Thorpe 'the hidden village,' and Linton with three bridges crossing its peaceful beck.

Burnsall is situated on a bend of the Wharfe where an impressive five-arched stone bridge spans the river. The village is noted for its classic fell race, held in mid-August. The race is to the summit of Burnsall Fell and back. It can be completed in under fifteen minutes by the best runners.

The present church, dating from 1150, was founded by St. Wilfred at the end of the seventh century. Inside are Viking hog-back tombstones, remains of Anglo-Saxon crosses and a Norman tub font. It also has an unusual lych-gate equipped with ropes and pulleys allowing it to swing on a central pivot.

The walk begins with a gentle stroll through the meadows below Kail Hill to the secluded hamlet of Thorpe.

Thorpe-sub-Montem, to give the village its full title, means 'below the hills.' It is hidden between the reef knolls of Kail Hill and Elbolton Hill. During the incursions by marauding Scots in the Middle Ages, dalesfolk came here to take refuge.

For centuries Thorpe was famous for high quality footwear. At one time over forty cobblers were employed making slippers, clogs and boots. On one occasion, in high spirits, they stole Burnsall's maypole and erected it on their own village green. Burnsall had to enlist help from the surrounding villages before descending on Thorpe. After a 'bloody' battle the maypole was victoriously carried back to Burnsall.

Both Kail Hill and Elbolton Hill are composed of pure limestone and are rich in fossils. In 1889, when Elbolton Cave was excavated, twelve Stone Age skeletons were found. They were in a sitting posture and partly fossilised. Remains of bears, wolves and giant elks have also been discovered there.

The route to Linton has several picturesque views, but unfortunately has to contend with the eyesore of the Swinden Quarry.

The Grange farmhouse at Linton has some well preserved bee boles. Until sugar became cheaper and readily available, beekeeping was common in the dales. Old fashioned hives, made from straw or wicker-work, were kept in recesses in walls, called 'boles.' They were normally about two feet square and eighteen inches deep, and usually faced south.

Linton's most prominent building is the Fountaine Hospital, built in 1721 and which was financed by bequests under the will of Richard Fountaine for 'six poor men and women.' An additional bequest of £26 per annum was to provide a coat or gown 'Blew lined with green.'

The Church of St. Michael and All Angels is situated half a mile away at Linton Falls, which is a sizeable hamlet in its own right. It is quite probable that the church occupies a former pagan site. These were usually built at the bends of rivers. The present structure dates from c1150 and the oldest parts are the Norman arches and the circular font. The building has a simple exterior with a broad low roof and a thirteenth century bell turret. The windows are a mixture of fourteenth and fifteenth century styles.

From the church a riverside path is followed back to Burnsall. This area is a haven for wildflowers; bluebells, bird's eye primroses, cranesbill, ragged robins and violets are some the many species to look out for. The river also attracts a wide variety of birdlife including mallards, dippers, herons, kingfishers, swallows, martins and oystercatchers.

Near Burnsall is the imposing limestone cliff of Loup Scar, the river here flows through a narrow gorge with near vertical sides. The heavily folded strata was created by the Craven Fault.

Start/Parking:	Burnsall, use either of the two car parks.
Location:	Burnsall is situated on the B6160 road 8 miles north east of Skipton.
Grid Ref:	032 611.
Distance:	7½ miles circular. Allow 3½ hrs.
OS Maps:	Outdoor Leisure Map 10 (1:25,000) or Landranger 98 (1:50,000).
Refreshments:	The Red Lion Inn, the Fell Hotel and the Wharfe View Tea rooms at Burnsall, the Fountaine Inn at Linton.
Public Toilets:	Burnsall and Linton Falls.
Other:	Bus service, shops, post office, telephone.

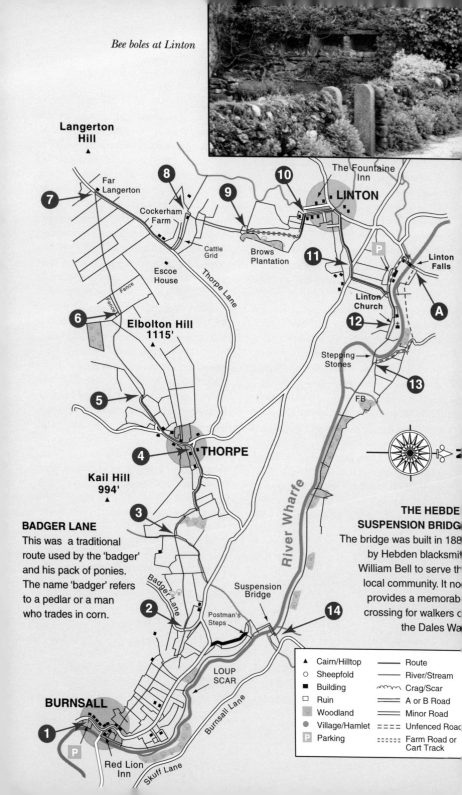

Bee boles at Linton

Langerton Hill ▲

7

Far Langerton

8

9

Cockerham Farm

Cattle Grid

Escoe House

Fence

Fence

6

Elbolton Hill
1115' ▲

5

Thorpe Lane

Brows Plantation

10

The Fountaine Inn

LINTON

P

11

Linton Falls

A

Linton Church

12

Stepping Stones

13

FB

4 **THORPE**

Kail Hill
994' ▲

3

BADGER LANE

This was a traditional route used by the 'badger' and his pack of ponies. The name 'badger' refers to a pedlar or a man who trades in corn.

2

Badger Lane

Postman's Steps

Suspension Bridge

River Wharfe

14

THE HEBDE
SUSPENSION BRIDG

The bridge was built in 188 by Hebden blacksmi William Bell to serve th local community. It no provides a memorab crossing for walkers o the Dales Wa

LOUP
SCAR

BURNSALL

1

P

Red Lion Inn

Burnsall Lane

Skuff Lane

▲	Cairn/Hilltop	▬▬	Route
o	Sheepfold	▬	River/Stream
■	Building	∿∿∿	Crag/Scar
□	Ruin	═══	A or B Road
	Woodland	══	Minor Road
●	Village/Hamlet	════	Unfenced Road
P	Parking	┄┄┄┄	Farm Road or Cart Track

2 Burnsall, Thorpe and Linton

1 *(GR 032 611)* From the car park, walk towards the Red Lion Inn. Turn left at the inn and go past the post office. Follow the road round a bend and go through a gate on the left *(SP Thorpe).* Continue down a narrow ginnel and through another gate. Follow a clear path leading through a series of stiles to Badger Lane.

2 *(GR 026 617)* Cross the lane and go through the stile opposite *(SP Thorpe).* Stay with the right wall for about fifty yards and then bear left *(SP footpath).* Continue through 3 stiles heading towards the left of a small wood.

3 *(GR 019 617)* Follow the right wall round to the back of the wood and climb up through a gate. Continue climbing with the left wall and go through a gate onto a farm track. Follow the track through a gate onto the road, Turn left and follow the road into Thorpe.

4 *(GR 013 618)* At the junction turn left and continue to another junction, Take the right fork *(SP Thorpe Lane)* and follow a walled track to Elbolton Hill.

5 *(GR 010 615)* Go through the gate, turn left and climb steeply uphill. At the wall corner go straight on keeping roughly to the same level to skirt round Elbolton Hill. Go through an open gateway, bear left and cross a ladder stile *(SP Footpath).*

6 *(GR 005 613)* Stay close to the fence, go through a gate and continue roughly in the same direction via 6 stiles to Thorpe Lane at Far Langerton.

7 *(GR 996 612)* Turn right and stay on the lane. After passing Cockerham farm turn left onto a walled track *(SP Linton/Threapland).* Go through a gate and descend to a barn.

8 *(GR 998 618)* Go through a stile in the right wall behind the barn. Continue via 2 gap stiles and then follow the right wall through 2 gates.

9 *(GR 999 622)* Join a clear farm track which descends through 2 gates into Linton. *(Look to the right of the farmhouse entrance to see the 'bee boles')*

10 *(GR 998 626)* From this gate follow the road through the village. Turn right at the junction and continue on the road, after about 30 yards turn right and follow a narrow tarmac lane which leads back to the main road.

11 *(GR 001 629)* Turn right and and stay on the road for about 70 yards. Leave the road over a stile on the left *(SP Linton Church and Falls),* follow a narrow fenced path leading down onto a tarmac lane at Linton Falls. Turn right and follow the lane through a gate to enter the grounds of Linton Church.

12 *(GR 005 632) See also blue panel below.* Follow a clear path through the churchyard and cross a stile in the right corner. Continue straight ahead to cross the river over some stepping stones. Climb up the bank towards a gate *(SP Burnsall and Hebden Mill).*

13 *(GR 008 631)* Bear right away from the gate and cross a small footbridge. Follow the river downstream to a suspension bridge at the foot of Hebden Gill.

14 *(GR 026 624)* Cross the bridge and turn left. Continue downstream to reach the road by the side of the Red Lion Inn at Burnsall Bridge. Return to the car park.

ALTERNATIVE PATH - to be used when the river is high.

12 *(GR 005 632)* Walk back along the lane going past the car park. Turn right at a signpost *(SP Footpath to Linton Falls)* and go down some steps. Follow a narrow lane round the back of the cottages to cross the wooden footbridge.

A *(GR 001 633)* Go through a gap stile on the right *(SP Hebden and Burnsall).* Continue downstream through 3 stiles onto a tarmac lane. Turn right and follow the lane past a trout farm after which the lane becomes a rough track. Go through a gate at the lane end.

GRASSINGTON MOOR and HEBDEN GILL

from Grassington (8¼ miles)

This rewarding walk has a variety of interests which reveal man's activities through the centuries. The contrast of terrain and scenery is excellent and the views are extensive.

Grassington, the capital of Upper Wharfedale, is one of the most charming villages in the Dales. In 1282, the village was granted charters to hold a market and three fairs. The market has long since gone and the last of the fairs, the Grassington Feast, petered out a few years ago. A traditional event was the children's 'tea cake eating race,' they had to eat a tea cake, run to the other end of the field, the first one to whistle a tune was the winner!

In 1349, the 'Black Death' struck Grassington, killing over twenty-five percent of the population. Despite this major setback the village slowly recovered and prosperity returned during the lead mining period of the eighteenth and nineteenth centuries.

From the village the route climbs over the shoulder of Kimpergill Hill. As height is gained panoramic views of the dale begin to unfold with Grass Wood directly below.

The path passes one of the most extensively developed Iron Age field systems in Britain, which covered an area of approximately 250 acres. It consists of square and rectangular fields which are clearly divided by stone and turf banks. There are also indications of a settlement. Outlines of hut circle foundations have been traced.

Continuing to Bare House there are dramatic views of the limestone pavements above Dib Scar. The large boulders perched on the skyline were left behind by the retreating glacier.

Bare House was first called Barras from the Norse 'Bargh-hus,' meaning 'hill farm.' The present building dates from the seventeenth century and is of a long house construction. This had a living area, a cow shed and a barn all under one roof.

The route continues along a walled track to Yarnbury, which was a thriving mining community until the late nineteenth century. At one time Yarnbury had a railway, a smithy, a weigh house and many miners' cottages.

The huge deposits of lead under Grassington Moor made it one of the most intensively mined areas in the dales. Large dams were constructed on the moor, linked by a complex network of water courses to the various buildings used to process the ore.

The mine workings covered a large area and exploration will be limited to time available. A visit to the Cupola smelt mill is strongly recommended. It was built in 1793 with twin furnaces, and twin flues which led 600 yards up the moor to twin chimneys 40 feet high. The mill was fired by coal and a continuous supply of ore was required to make it economical. It processed ore until 1886 when cheap imports forced the mines to close.

The journey to Hebden follows the course of the delightful Hebden Beck leaving the desolation of the mines behind. Just below Hole Bottom is the striking waterfall of Scala Force.

Hebden enjoys an elevated position overlooking the green, tree-lined Hebden Gill. There is a spring in the village known as Thurskill's Well. According to local legend, this ancient well is dedicated to Thor, the Norse God of War. The well is presently used as a water supply for a fish farm.

Former inhabitants of Hebden had a reputation for being unable to pronounce *th* which they rendered as *f*. Their epic example was "I fink I fought I heard it funner, free fousand free hundred and firty-free times above Forpe Fell End."

During the return to Grassington there are extensive views across the dale to Barden Moor, Simon's Seat, Thorpe Fell and *once again* the unsightly Swinden Quarry!

Start/Parking:	Grassington YDNP car park on the B6265 Pateley Bridge road.
Location:	Grassington is situated 10 miles north east of Skipton. Leave the B6160 at Threshfield and follow the B6265.
Grid Ref:	002 638.
Distance:	8¼ miles circular. Allow 4½ hrs.
OS Maps:	Outdoor Leisure Map 10 (1:25,000) or Landranger 98 (1:50,000).
Refreshments:	Several pubs, tea rooms and a fish shop at Grassington. The Clarendon Hotel at Hebden.
Public Toilets:	Grassington and Hebden.
Other:	Post office, telephone, bus service, shops, museum.

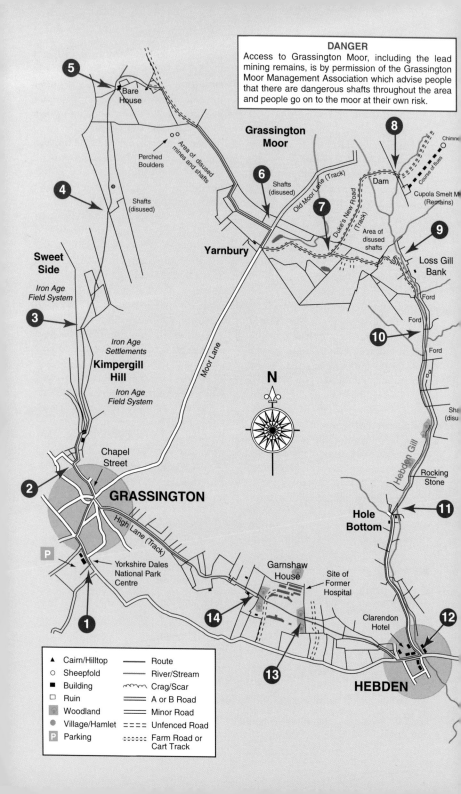

DANGER

Access to Grassington Moor, including the lead mining remains, is by permission of the Grassington Moor Management Association which advise people that there are dangerous shafts throughout the area and people go on to the moor at their own risk.

5

Bare House

Perched Boulders

Area of disused mines and shafts

Grassington Moor

8

Chimney

4

Shafts (disused)

6

Shafts (disused)

Old Moor Lane (Track)

Duke's New Road (Track)

Dam

Course of flues

Cupola Smelt Mill (Remains)

Sweet Side

Iron Age Field System

3

7

Yarnbury

Area of disused shafts

9

Loss Gill Bank

Ford

Iron Age Settlements

Kimpergill Hill

Iron Age Field System

Moor Lane

Ford

10

Ford

N

Sha (disu

Hebden Gill

Chapel Street

2

GRASSINGTON

Rocking Stone

Hole Bottom

11

High Lane (Track)

P

Yorkshire Dales National Park Centre

Garnshaw House

Site of Former Hospital

Clarendon Hotel

12

1

14

13

HEBDEN

▲	Cairn/Hilltop	──	Route
○	Sheepfold	──	River/Stream
■	Building	〜〜〜	Crag/Scar
□	Ruin	══	A or B Road
	Woodland	══	Minor Road
●	Village/Hamlet	====	Unfenced Road
P	Parking	······	Farm Road or Cart Track

3 Grassington Moor and Hebden Gill

1 *(GR 002 638)* From the car park entrance turn left and follow the road. Turn right into Main Street, keep to the left of the cobbled square and go past the Devonshire Arms. Turn left into Chapel Street and continue to Bank Lane.

2 *(GR 002 644)* Turn right *(SP Bare House/Bycliffe Road)* and follow a tarmac lane uphill. Turn left. The lane soon levels out and becomes a rough track. After passing a stable block turn right onto a green lane and cross a wooden stile. Bear left, continue through a long pasture and go through a stile.

3 *(GR 003 653)* Bear half right and cross a ladder stile. Bear left, cross 2 broken walls and a step stile. Cross the next pasture, in roughly the same direction, to a ladder stile.

4 *(GR 004 661)* Go over the stile, bear half left and climb a small hill where the track levels out. Continue past an enclosure, bear right following a track over another small hill and go through a stile. Stay on the same heading to arrive at Bare House.

5 *(GR 005 669)* Go through the gate *(SP Conistone)*. Turn right and follow the wall round to a gate at the side of a barn. Go through the gate and head diagonally across the field to join a clear track. Turn right and follow the track through a gate where it becomes enclosed. Follow this track which leads to Yarnbury.

6 *(GR 016 660)* Turn right and follow the road for about 120 yards. Leave the road through a gate on the left *(SP Hebden)* and continue ahead on a broad track passing some spoil heaps and a line of bell pits to a T-junction.

7 *(GR 020 658)* *To visit the leadmine remains* - Turn left and follow the track uphill *(The Duke's New Road)*. Go over a ladder stile and descend to cross an old dam. Continue on the track climbing back up, and go over another ladder stile.

8 *(GR 025 664)* Turn right to visit the remains of the Cupola Smelt Mill. Return by the same route to the T-junction at point 7. Turn left and go through an open gateway. Continue through a gate and follow the track to the left *(SP Bridleway)* descending to Hebden Gill.

9 *(GR 025 658)* Turn right onto a good track, pass an old limekiln and go through an open gateway. Cross the gill at a ford and about 100 yards further on recross the gill at another ford, continue along the gill to a gate

10 *(GR 026 654)* Continue through the gate and after 50 yards cross the gill at a ford. A good track now leads through 4 gates and over a small bridge to reach Hole Bottom.

11 *(GR 024 641)* Go through the gate, bear left and follow the narrow lane through 2 gates to Hebden village.

12 *(GR 026 632)* Turn right at the main road and go past the Clarendon Hotel. Turn right and follow an enclosed track *(SP To Grassington via High Lane)*. Cross a stone stile. Follow the left wall, go over a step stile and continue across 2 fields to enter a wood.

13 *(GR 018 634)* Continue ahead *(SP Grassington)* and go straight across the field. At a junction of tarmac paths continue straight ahead *(SP footpath)* leaving the tarmac path. Go through another wood, crossing a service road and leave the wood over a stile.

14 *(GR 015 636)* Stay with the left wall through 3 more stiles. Bear left onto a clear track and go through a gated stile. Stay with the right wall to its corner. Bear right and cross a wooden step stile in the far right corner onto an enclosed track. At the end of the track turn right and continue to Main Street. Turn left and return to the car park via the outward route.

CONISTONE DIB
and DIB SCAR

from Grassington (7 miles)

Starting from Grassington this outstanding walk follows well defined paths and has a few easy climbs. The views throughout the walk are excellent and the archaeological content is intriguing.

Part of Grassington's charm has to be attributed to its many hidden alleyways or 'folds' leading off the cobbled market square and the main street. The 'folds,' with names such as Jakey, Chamber End Fold, Plett's Fold, The Woggins and Horse Gap Yett, were once Anglian crofts. Over the years they have become tightly packed with houses. Many of these were built to provide homes for miners and their families during the eighteenth and nineteenth centuries.

Two converted miners' cottages now house the Upper Wharfedale Folk Museum. It has many reminders of the past, with exhibits of minerals, dales farming, lead mining, folk lore, period costumes and domestic life of the area. The museum also recalls the days of the Yorkshire Dales Railway which reached Grassington in 1902.

The railway stimulated tourism and industry, helping to stop the decline in population of Upper Wharfedale by bringing Bradford businessmen to live in the area. The line was a branch of the old Midland Railway from Skipton to Grassington. Proposals were made to continue the line under Great Whernside, through Coverdale and on to Darlington. These had to be shelved because the expense was too great. The line closed to passenger traffic in 1930 due to the increasing competition from bus services.

The Dales Way footpath is followed from the village to the large pasture of Lea Green. The route passes a line of shallow, fifteenth century lead mining shafts known as 'coffin workings.' The records of Fountains Abbey show that the monks purchased lead from these mines in 1484. At the centre of Lea Green is a Bronze Age burial mound, measuring 76 feet by 66 feet. Seven burials took place within the mound and excavations have uncovered four iron knives, a bronze pin, a bronze razor and a bone pin.

One of the largest Iron Age sites in England is to be found at the northern end of Lea Green. This was occupied from c200 BC to cAD 400 and would have been an important Brigantian settlement. Finds of bone spoons, iron sickles and knives, pottery and many other artifacts have been made here. The dewpond is fed by a natural spring and has supplied water to grazing animals for generations. Its exact age is uncertain, but the funnelling walls were built in 1822.

The clear path to Conistone allows time to enjoy the excellent limestone scenery. Conistone Dib is a dry valley carved by glacial meltwaters. At the end of the Ice Age the ground was still frozen hard, preventing water from sinking down. Vast amounts of water from the melting ice rushed down the steep slopes cutting wedge shaped gorges into the valley sides. As the climate warmed up the ground thawed out and the water sank underground leaving the gorges dry.

Conistone is a very attractive little village sited peacefully away from the main valley road. It is of eighth century Anglian origin and its name means 'the king's farm.' The church was almost completely rebuilt in 1846 but is thought to have Saxon foundations. The two west arches and the font are Norman.

The route from Conistone climbs to Dib Scar, another fine example of a dry valley. After returning to Lea Green Pasture the path crosses a small limestone pavement and continues to Grassington by the outward route.

Limestone pavements were formed by the glaciers scraping the land down to bare limestone. Further erosion by rainwater produced a network of blocks (clints) and crevices (grykes). The damp, sheltered grykes provide a refuge for woodland plants, including rock roses, mountain pansies and several rare ferns.

Start/Parking:	Grassington YDNP car park on the B6265 Pateley Bridge road.
Location:	Grassington is situated 10 miles north east of Skipton. Leave the B6160 at Threshfield and follow the B6265.
Grid Ref:	002 638.
Distance:	7 miles circular. Allow 3½ hrs.
OS Maps:	Outdoor Leisure Map 10 (1:25,000) or Landranger 98 (1:50,000).
Refreshments:	Several pubs, tea rooms and a fish shop at Grassington.
Public Toilets:	Grassington.
Other:	Post office, telephone, bus service, shops, museum.

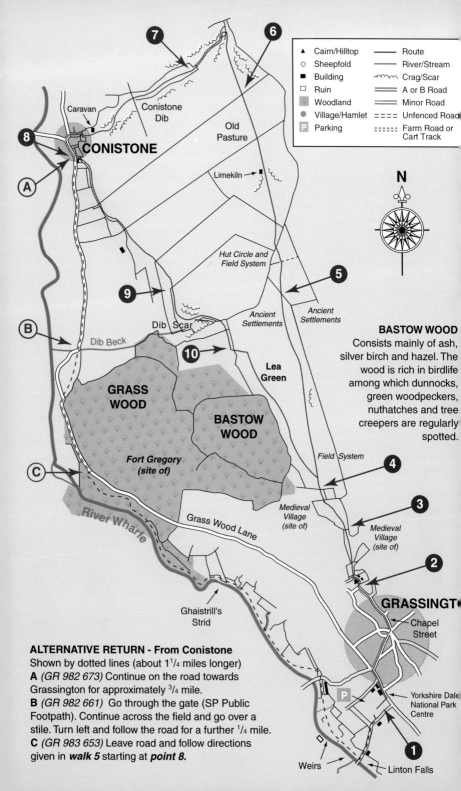

Map Legend

Symbol	Description	Symbol	Description
▲	Cairn/Hilltop	——	Route
○	Sheepfold	——	River/Stream
■	Building	⌒⌒⌒	Crag/Scar
□	Ruin	═══	A or B Road
▨	Woodland	═══	Minor Road
●	Village/Hamlet	====	Unfenced Road
P	Parking	::::::	Farm Road or Cart Track

Caravan

Conistone Dib

CONISTONE

Old Pasture

Limekiln →

Hut Circle and Field System

Ancient Settlements

Ancient Settlements

Dib Scar

Dib Beck

GRASS WOOD

Lea Green

BASTOW WOOD

BASTOW WOOD

Consists mainly of ash, silver birch and hazel. The wood is rich in birdlife among which dunnocks, green woodpeckers, nuthatches and tree creepers are regularly spotted.

Fort Gregory (site of)

Field System

River Wharfe

Grass Wood Lane

Medieval Village (site of)

Medieval Village (site of)

Ghaistrill's Strid

GRASSINGTON

Chapel Street

P

Yorkshire Dales National Park Centre

Weirs

Linton Falls

ALTERNATIVE RETURN - From Conistone
Shown by dotted lines (about 1¼ miles longer)
A *(GR 982 673)* Continue on the road towards Grassington for approximately ¾ mile.
B *(GR 982 661)* Go through the gate (SP Public Footpath). Continue across the field and go over a stile. Turn left and follow the road for a further ¼ mile.
C *(GR 983 653)* Leave road and follow directions given in *walk 5* starting at *point 8*.

4 Conistone Dib and Dib Scar

1 *(GR 002 638)* From the car park entrance turn left and follow the road. Turn right into Main Street, keep to the left of the cobbled square and go past the Devonshire Arms. Turn left into Chapel Street, follow the lane to a sharp left bend.

2 *(GR 001 645)* Leave the lane via a farmyard on the right *(SP Conistone)*. Pass to the right of the main building, turn left at a stable block *(SP Conistone/Grass Wood)*. Pass between the farm buildings and leave the farmyard through a gate behind a storage tank. Follow the path to the right *(SP Conistone)* and go through a gate *(SP Footpath)*. Continue on a clear track to a gap stile.

3 *(GR 001 649)* Go through the stile and bear left onto a clear track which descends at first before climbing back up towards the right of the wood. Go through a gap stile and follow the right wall to cross a stone step stile.

4 *(GR 999 651)* Continue straight ahead ignoring all side paths and climb around the hill on the right. Follow a clear track which descends to cross a ladder stile.

5 *(GR 996 664)* Bear left onto a broad track, cross a collapsed wall and go through a gate. Turn right, follow the right wall and cross a ladder stile. Continue in the same direction. Pass a limekiln and cross 2 more ladder stiles.

6 *(GR 994 678)* Bear right *(SP Kettlewell)* heading towards the top of Conistone Dib. Go over a ladder stile in the left wall *(SP Conistone)*, turn left and scramble down a narrow cleft to enter the Dib. Cross a ladder stile and stay with the right wall descending to cross another ladder stile.

7 *(GR 990 679)* Continue downhill, cross a ladder stile and pass through a narrow gorge to enter Conistone via a gate. Continue down to the main road. Turn left and follow the road towards Grassington.

8 *(GR 982 673)* About 50 yards past the Youth Hostel turn left onto a stony track *(SP Grassington)*. Go through a gate and continue uphill via 4 more gates.

9 *(GR 989 665)* Stay with the right wall. When the track becomes rougher, bear left and follow the waymark posts. Continue with the right wall to cross a stone step stile *(SP Grassington)*. Cross a small ravine at Dib Scar and climb the hill opposite, stay with the left wall to a ladder stile.

10 *(GR 993 661)* Cross the stile and turn right. Follow the wall for about 150 yards and bear left onto a clear path which stays roughly 75 yards from the right wall. The track leads to the stone step stile crossed at Point 4. Return to Grassington by the outward route.

Conistone Dib

GRASS WOOD
and GHAISTRILL'S STRID

from Grassington (5¼ miles)

This is a relaxing short walk from Grassington visiting the flower rich Grass Wood. The return along the riverside is well known for its variety of wild birds.

Grass Wood is an important nature reserve, covering an area of over 250 acres. It is sited on a mass of great scar limestone and has been credited with between 300 and 400 species of wildflowers, many of them very rare. The wood is managed by the Yorkshire Wildlife Trust which has added a selection of hardwoods and conifers to the established ash and birch woodland. Coppicing and selective felling have been introduced to encourage the growth of the natural species of trees and re-establish ground flora.

Near the entrance to the wood is an ancient Iron Age settlement. Although it is now difficult to make out, several circular dwellings were dug out of the hillside to a depth of about five feet. The rock face was used for the rear wall and then rubble walls were built in a rough circle to give an internal diameter of about ten feet. The walls tapered towards the top, indicating that they are likely to have had stone roofs and a central hearth. The entrance was through a narrow passage seven feet long.

The path climbs gently from the settlement site and a signpost points the way to Fort Gregory. This was a Brigantian stronghold and played an important role in resisting the Roman

26

onslaught in AD 74. The fort is sited on a limestone plateau 350 feet above the River Wharfe and commands superb views of the valley. The summit was enclosed by a wall approximately 500 feet by 200 feet where livestock and cattle were kept during hostilities. The Brigantes were eventually subdued by the might of the Roman army. Many were enslaved to prevent further insurrections and some were put to work in the lead mines.

Grass Wood has a darker side. Here in 1766, Dr. Petty of Grassington was brutally murdered by Tom Lee, the village blacksmith. Lee was also a poacher, and the doctor, who had occasionally attended to his wounds, suspected him of other crimes in the area. Fearing that the doctor would inform the authorities, Lee made plans to get rid of him. One night when Dr. Petty was returning home from Kilnsey, Lee lay in wait by the entrance to Grass Wood. As soon as the doctor entered the wood he was knocked to the ground and savagely killed. Lee hid the body, first in the wood, then in a peat bog on the moor. Finally, he threw it into the river at Loup Scar near Burnsall. It was two years before Tom Lee was brought to justice at York Assizes, where he was found guilty and hanged. His body was returned to Grassington and hung in chains from a gibbet in Grass Wood.

From the wood a beautiful stretch of the River Wharfe leads to the narrow gorge at Ghaistrill's Strid. Here the river is a turbulent series of rapids and its banks well known for its wildflowers and birds. The riverside path continues to Grassington Bridge. This was built in 1603 and is the oldest bridge across the Wharfe, having escaped the flood of 1673. It was widened in 1780 and raised to its present level in 1825. Underneath the arches the two stages of building can be seen and the older section bears masons' marks.

After crossing the road, the path is followed to the 'Tin Bridge' at Linton Falls. The name refers to the original bridge which was built in 1814. It was covered with sheets of tin from old oil drums to stop the wearing away of the timber. The present bridge was built in 1989 by the Royal Engineers and is expected to last for 150 years.

From here, a narrow, walled path is followed leading back to the car park. This path is known locally as 'The Snake Walk.'

Start/Parking:	Grassington YDNP car park on the B6265 Pateley Bridge road.
Location:	Grassington is situated 10 miles north east of Skipton. Leave the B6160 at Threshfield and follow the B6265.
Grid Ref:	002 638.
Distance:	5¼ miles circular. Allow 3 hrs.
OS Maps:	Outdoor Leisure Map 10 (1:25,000) or Landranger 98 (1:50,000).
Refreshments:	Several pubs, tea rooms and a fish shop at Grassington.
Public Toilets:	Grassington.
Other:	Post office, telephone, bus service, shops, museum.

Grass Wood

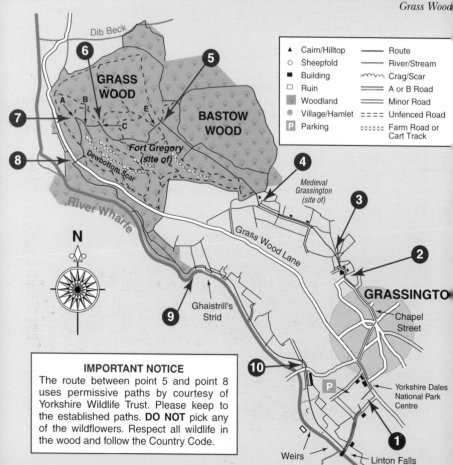

Dib Beck

GRASS WOOD

BASTOW WOOD

Fort Gregory
(site of)

Dewbottom Scar

River Wharfe

Medieval
Grassington
(site of)

Grass Wood Lane

GRASSINGTO

Chapel
Street

Ghaistrill's
Strid

Yorkshire Dales
National Park
Centre

Weirs

Linton Falls

Symbol	Legend	Symbol	Legend
▲	Cairn/Hilltop	——	Route
○	Sheepfold	——	River/Stream
■	Building	═══	Crag/Scar
□	Ruin	═══	A or B Road
▦	Woodland	═══	Minor Road
●	Village/Hamlet	====	Unfenced Road
P	Parking	⋮⋮⋮⋮	Farm Road or Cart Track

IMPORTANT NOTICE

The route between point 5 and point 8 uses permissive paths by courtesy of Yorkshire Wildlife Trust. Please keep to the established paths. **DO NOT** pick any of the wildflowers. Respect all wildlife in the wood and follow the Country Code.

5 Grass Wood and Ghaistrill's Strid

1 *(GR 002 638)* From the car park entrance turn left and follow the road. Turn right into Main Street, keep to the left of the cobbled square and go past the Devonshire Arms. Turn left into Chapel Street, follow the lane to a sharp left bend.

2 *(GR 001 645)* Leave the lane via a farmyard on the right *(SP Conistone)*. Pass to the right of the main building, turn left at a stable block *(SP Conistone/Grass Wood)*. Pass between the farm buildings and leave the farmyard through a gate behind a storage tank. Follow the path to the left *(SP Footpath to Grass Wood)*.

3 *(GR 001 646)* Go through a gap stile *(SP Footpath)* and continue downhill to the right of a tree. Go through a gap stile onto a walled lane. Continue directly ahead along the walled lane and go through a gate into a narrow field. Cross the field to another gate.

4 *(GR 995 650)* Go through the gate and cross the field to a ladderstile leading into Grass Wood. Continue straight ahead and climb gently uphill to arrive at a signpost.

5 *(GR 989 655)* Turn left and follow a rough track *(SP Fort Gregory)*. Cross the forest trail at **marker post E** and climb to the site of the fort *(Fort Gregory AD70)*. Cross the summit and descend to another forest trail. Turn right and follow this trail ignoring all side tracks to **marker post C.**

6 *(GR 984 655)* Turn Left and follow the path to **marker post B**. To visit the viewpoint at Dewbottom Scar, turn left and follow the path for about 10 yards. Return to **marker post B** and continue straight ahead descending to **marker post A**.

7 *(GR 982 655)* Turn sharp left and descend steeply to join a track coming from the right. Follow this path for about 10 yards and turn right onto a clear path leading down to the road

8 *(GR 983 653)* Cross the road and go through the gate opposite *(SP Grassington)*. Bear left and follow a clear path leading through the wood which eventually drops down to the river. Cross a wooden stile and then follow the riverside downstream to Ghaistrill's Strid.

9 *(GR 991 645)* At Ghaistrill's Strid pass through a combination of 4 stiles and 2 gates. Continue downstream and go through a gate and over a bridge. After the next gate bear left away from the river and go through a gate leading up the main road.

10 *(GR 999 639)* Cross the road and go through a gate opposite *(SP Hebden/Burnsall)*. Continue on a clear path and cross a plank bridge heading towards the river. At the wooden bridge go through a gap stile. Turn left and follow a narrow walled track up via 2 gates and then go through a gate on the left leading back into the car park.

The weirs near Linton Falls

6

THE MONK'S ROAD and HAWKSWICK COTE

from Arncliffe (10 miles)

Following two ancient tracks, this moderate hill walk introduces some of Littondale's finest scenery. It briefly visits Malhamdale, famous for its 'Tarn' and 'Cove.'

Arncliffe is the largest settlement in Littondale, a very attractive village, surrounded by unrivalled limestone scenery. It is Saxon in origin and the name means 'the eagle's cliff,' which suggests that birds of prey once nested in the nearby scars.

The village has a large rectangular green enclosed by stone houses, farms and barns. At the far corner of the green stands 'The Falcon Inn,' where ale is still served up in a jug directly from the cask. The inn was once kept by Marmaduke Miller, a local wood engraver and noted water colourist, and it is still run by his descendants. Arncliffe was the first location for the television series *Emmerdale Farm*, with the inn featuring as 'The Woolpack.'

The local scenery inspired Charles Kingsley, during his stay at Arncliffe in 1863, to write his novel *The Water Babies*. Littondale became Vendale and Tom, the boy in the story, supposedly met the water babies in a pool under the bridge near the church. The book condemned the practice of using small boys as chimney sweeps.

Leaving the village, a walled track at the side of the inn, leads past the old schoolhouse before climbing the hillside to join the Monk's Road. This former pack horse route links Malham to Arncliffe and was developed by the monasteries to gather the produce from their far reaching estates. They created a market for cereals, meat, linen, wool and footwear. As monastic trade increased so did the prosperity of the local villages. Some such as Kettlewell became early market towns.

The track to Dew Bottoms provides good views of the V-shaped valley of Cowside Beck which is a fine example of a valley created by water erosion.

Dew Bottoms is the site of an early Iron Age settlement consisting of five small fields, four circular huts and two rectangular ones. The borders of the fields are defined by low stone and turf banks which were the foundations for a timber stockade. The site could have been in use during the Bronze Age and fragments of pottery from that period have been found.

The first sign of recent civilisation is at Middle House, a seventeenth century farmhouse skillfully restored in 1990 by the National Trust. The site is possibly of Norse origin and until the sixteenth century it was a grange farm belonging to Fountains Abbey. The monks raised sheep on these granges. Much of the wool they produced was exported to Europe.

On the approach to Great Close Pasture the views across Malhamdale are very impressive. In the eighteenth century this peaceful pasture hosted one of the largest livestock markets in the north. Scottish cattle and sheep were gathered here to be bought and sold before continuing their journey to the expanding industrial towns of the West Riding and Lancashire.

From Great Close another ancient track leads over the summit. It then returns to Littondale. The limestone scenery from the summit is impressive with white scars rising in all directions. On the descent to Hawkswick Cote there are excellent views of Buckden Pike and Great Whernside.

Peregrine falcons have recently been re-established in this part of the dale. Soaring high above their intended prey, peregrines 'stoop' or dive at speeds of up to 180 mph, often striking in mid-air and killing their prey with a sharp blow. The peregrine is one of nature's swiftest and most beautiful birds of prey. The name is from the Latin peregrinus, meaning 'foreigner' or 'traveller.'

The return to Arncliffe follows a delightful path alongside the River Skirfare, well known for its birdlife, trout fishing and wildflowers.

Start/Parking:	Arncliffe village, parking on the road alongside the green.
Location:	Arncliffe is located 15 miles north of Skipton. Leave the B6160 after passing Kilnsey signposted Arncliffe 3 miles.
Grid Ref:	931 718.
Distance:	10 miles circular. Allow 5½ hrs.
OS Maps:	Outdoor Leisure Map 10 (1:25,000) or Landranger 98 (1:50,000).
Refreshments:	The Falcon Inn and Raikes Cottage Tea Rooms at Arncliffe.
Public Toilets:	None on route.
Other:	Post office, telephone.

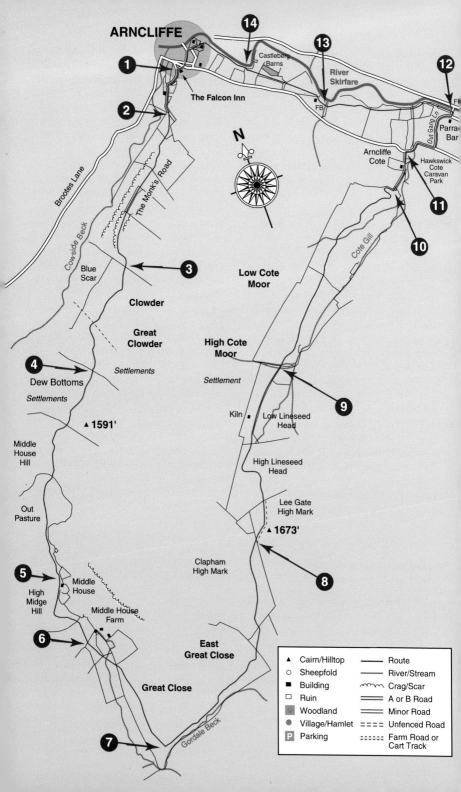

6   The Monk's Road and Hawkswick Cote

1   *(GR 931 718)* Leave Arncliffe along a walled lane at the side of the Falcon Hotel *(SP Malham)*. Follow the lane past the old School House to a gated stile.

2   *(GR 929 715)* Go through the stile *(SP Malham)*, climb up the hillside and cross a ladder stile to join the Monk's Road. Continue climbing gradually and cross a further 4 ladder stiles.

3   *(GR 921 704)* Continue on a cairned path, go through a broken wall and cross a ladder stile to reach Dew Bottoms.

4   *(GR 916 697)* Go straight ahead from the stile. Follow a clear track over two more ladder stiles. Stay on the track across Out Pasture returning to the wallside. Follow the wall to Middle House.

5   *(GR 907 682)* Go past the farm house and follow a rough track to the wall corner, stay on the track which sweeps round and descends to cross a ladder stile. Continue down to cross a wooden step stile onto the farm road at Middle House Farm.

6   *(GR 907 676)* From the stile head towards a gate in the top left corner of the field *(SP Street Gate)*. Go through the gate and continue to cross a ladder stile into Great Close Pasture. Turn right and follow a faint path across the pasture keeping the right wall in sight.

7   *(GR 911 665)* Turn left and begin a steady climb following the right wall up to go through a gate. Bear left dropping down slightly and go through a gate. Bear right and follow a clear track climbing up to go through a gate in the right wall.

8   *(GR 924 679)* Follow a broken wall round and go through a gate. Continue ahead and then begin descending through 2 gates to the head of Cote Gill.

9   *(GR 931 692)* Follow a clear track leading away from the edge of the gill and go through a gate. Continue in roughly the same direction winding down to a gate.

10   *(GR 946 702)* Go through a gate and cross a ladder stile onto a narrow walled track. Follow the track down through another gate, go past the farmhouse at Arncliffe Cote and continue through a gate onto the main road.

11   *(GR 947 705)* Turn right, follow the road round a double bend passing the Hawkswick Cote Caravan Site. Turn left onto a narrow single track road which leads to Hawkswick. Follow the lane to a barn, turn left *(SP Arncliffe)* and follow a narrow walled track towards a footbridge over the river. **DON'T** cross the bridge!

12   *(GR 952 707)* Go over a ladder stile on the left *(SP Arncliffe)*. Continue along the riverside cross a wooden step stile, a gated stile and then another wooden step stile leaving the riverside. Turn right and follow a clear path across 4 meadows to a footbridge.

13   *(GR 942 711)* Cross the footbridge/stile combination and bear right and go through a gate. Turn left and continue through 2 gap stiles *(over a walled lane)*. Continue over 2 ladder stiles returning to the riverside.

14   *(GR 937 716)* Follow a clear waymarked path upstream to enter Arncliffe near St. Oswald's Church. Turn left and follow the road back to the village green.

BIRKS FELL, LITTONDALE and OLD COTE MOOR

from Buckden (11¼ miles)

This is a strenuous hill walk with some exceptional panoramic views. Sufficient time should be allowed to savour the many species of birds and wildflowers, the villages and the inns.

Buckden's bridge was built in 1750, with money granted for the rebuilding of Hubberholme's bridge which had been washed away two years earlier. It became known as the 'election bridge' after the parliamentary candidate had promised the new bridge to Buckden in exchange for their votes. Hubberholme's bridge became a 'ladder not worth ten groats.'

The route from the village climbs over the ridge at Firth Fell following the former corpse way. Until the latter half of the fifteenth century Hubberholme's church was only a chapel of ease and all burials had to take place at Arncliffe church. One record tells of a corpse being lost in the swollen River Wharfe, another of eight bearers who almost perished in deep snow.

The summit of Birks Fell lies about one mile to the north of the track but there is no right of way to it. However, the views across Littondale from Firth Fell do help to compensate for this inconvenience. Penyghent, Fountains Fell, Whernside, High Seat and Great Shunner Fell are embraced in one sweep. On a clear day the tops of the higher lakeland fells are also visible.

After a steep descent, a delightful green lane leads into Litton emerging near the Queen's Arms Inn. Litton is a quiet village now, but it was notorious in the eighteenth century for its cockpit, known as 'Fighting Cock's Croft.' It was here that Tom Lee, the infamous Grass Wood's murderer, brought his fighting cock to challenge the Litton cock. After his bird lost, Lee refused to accept the verdict or settle his bets and so he was ducked in the river and driven out of the village.

The route to Arncliffe reveals the valley's distinctive U-shaped trough. Littondale is a glacial valley with a broad, flat floor and steep sided limestone scars. It has a variety of natural woodland. Scoska Wood is the largest ash and rowan wood left in the dales.

In Scoska Cave, above the wood, the skeleton of a Bronze Age woman was discovered together with pottery and other items. She had suffered a fractured skull, possibly the result of being struck with a club.

In 1968, excavations at the earthwork near Thornsber Barn uncovered a Roman coin minted in AD 243, an iron knife, sherds of coarse pottery and animal bones. The D-shaped site measures 165 feet by 148 feet in three stepped terraces and is part of a larger field system.

Arncliffe is the largest village in the dale and also the most beautiful. Many of the houses surrounding the green are Grade II listed buildings and most of the village is a conservation area.

The church, dedicated to St. Oswald, was founded in the twelfth century and is peacefully situated by the side of the River Skirfare. It was rebuilt in 1796, apart from its fifteenth century tower. Further restoration was undertaken in 1841 giving the church its present charm. The church has one of the oldest bells in the country, dated 1350. It was probably a gift from Fountains Abbey. A list inside records the names of thirty-four Littondale men who fought alongside Henry Clifford, the 'Shepherd Lord,' at the Battle of Flodden Field in 1513. There is also a pike which may have been used in the battle and a silver chalice made in 1619.

The track across Old Cote Moor is a continuation of the Monk's Road, *(see walk 6)*, leading to Starbotton and then on to Coverdale. The views from Old Cote Moor include Buckden Pike and Great Whernside.

The easy return to Buckden follows the Dales Way with some striking river scenery along the way.

Start/Parking:	Buckden YDNP car park.
Location:	Buckden is situated on the B6160 4 miles north of Kettlewell and 18 miles north of Skipton.
Grid Ref:	942 773.
Distance:	11¼ miles circular. Allow 6½ hrs.
OS Maps:	Outdoor Leisure Map 30 (1:25,000) or Landranger 98 (1:50,000).
Refreshments:	The Buck Inn and the Village Tea Rooms at Buckden, The Queen's Arms at Litton, The Falcon Inn and Raikes Cottage Tea Rooms at Arncliffe, The Fox and Hounds at Starbotton.
Public Toilets:	Buckden near the entrance to the YDNP car park.
Other:	Post office, telephone, limited bus service, shops.

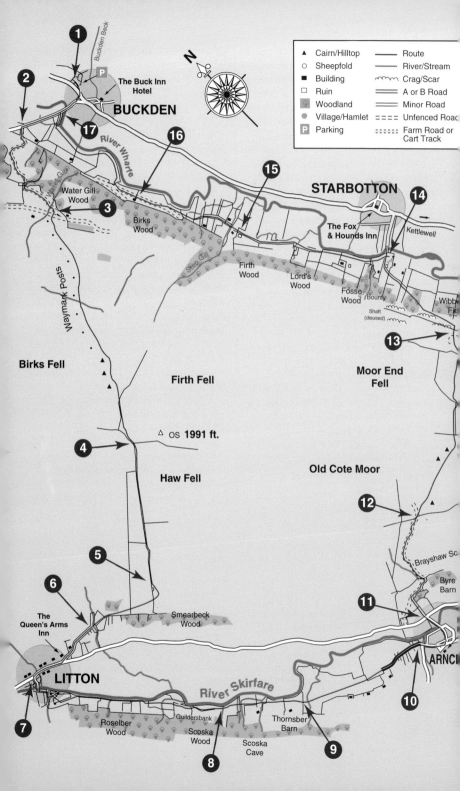

Legend

▲	Cairn/Hilltop		⎯⎯	Route
○	Sheepfold		⎯⎯	River/Stream
■	Building		⌒⌒⌒	Crag/Scar
□	Ruin		═══	A or B Road
▦	Woodland		⎯⎯	Minor Road
●	Village/Hamlet		====	Unfenced Road
P	Parking		⋯⋯⋯	Farm Road or Cart Track

N

① ②

Buckden Beck

P

The Buck Inn Hotel

BUCKDEN

⑰

River Wharfe

⑯

Webb Gill

Water Gill Wood

③

Birks Wood

⑮

Step Gill

Firth Wood

Lord's Wood

STARBOTTON

⑭

The Fox & Hounds Inn

Kettlewell

Fosse Wood

Bounty

Wibb Fie

Shaft (disused)

⑬

Waymark Posts

Birks Fell

Firth Fell

△ OS **1991 ft.**

Moor End Fell

④

Haw Fell

Old Cote Moor

⑫

Brayshaw Sc

Byre Barn

⑤

⑪

⑥

Smearbeck Wood

The Queen's Arms Inn

ARNC

⑩

River Skirfare

LITTON

⑦

Roselber Wood

Guildersbank

Thornsber Barn

⑨

⑧

Scoska Wood

Scoska Cave

7 Birks Fell, Littondale and Old Cote Moor

1 *(GR 942 773)* Leave the car park by the entrance. Turn left, after a few yards cross the road and follow a rough track down to the Hubberholme road. Turn right, follow the road over the river bridge and continue towards Hubberholme.

2 *(GR 936 775)* Turn left onto a farm road *(SP Litton)* and cross a cattle grid. Bear right onto a rougher track and continue uphill through 2 gates to the open moor. Turn left and follow the track to a signpost *(SP Bridleway)*.

3 *(GR 934 768)* Leave the track and follow a waymarked path uphill. Go through a gap in the wall and continue with the right wall to a gate on the summit.

4 *(GR 924 749)* Go through the gate and continue on a level track for about 150 yards. Stay close to the wall and begin descending steeply through another gate.

5 *(GR 917 740)* Bear left and follow a clear track sweeping back through a gap in the wall. Continue descending via 3 gates, over a bridge and join an enclosed lane.

6 *(GR 911 741)* Follow the lane through a gate, go through a farmyard and continue to the road near the Queen's Arms. Turn right and follow the road past the telephone box.

7 *(GR 904 742)* Turn left *(SP Bridleway)*. Follow a narrow lane and cross the river over a footbridge. Turn left, go through a gap stile, a gate and across a beck. Bear left onto a farm lane and go through a gate on the right *(SP Arncliffe)*. Cross the field and turn left *(SP Arncliffe)*. Continue to the wall corner, bear left *(SP footpath)* and go through a gate returning to the river. Follow a clear path downstream.

8 *(GR 915 728)* Leave the river, bearing right to go over a ladder stile. Cross two meadows and go over another ladder stile returning to the riverside.

9 *(GR 920 723)* From this gate leave the riverside, cross a large meadow and go through a stile. Continue via a gate onto an enclosed lane leading to Arncliffe.

10 *(GR 930 720)* Follow the road past the Falcon Inn. Turn left at the disused water pump and follow a narrow lane to a junction. Continue over the river bridge to a T-junction.

11 *(GR 932 721)* Go through a stile in the wall *(SP Starbotton)*. Follow the right wall up through another stile to join a clear track. Turn right and continue via 2 gates to reach the open moor.

12 *(GR 937 727)* Bear right and continue climbing on a cairned track. Cross a ladder stile to reach the summit. Continue with the right wall and begin descending. Go through a gap in the wall and continue down through 2 pastures.

13 *(GR 951 736)* Go through the gate *(SP Starbotton)*. Turn left, follow a clear path descending through a wood and crossing several broken walls. Turn right at a ruined barn and continue to a junction of paths by a signpost.

14 *(GR 951 745)* Turn left *(SP Buckden)* and follow the river upstream. Cross a small footbridge and continue over 2 stiles. At this point the path leaves the river and stays close to the left wall.

15 *(GR 944 755)* Cross a ladder stile by a ruined barn, continue through a gate and over a footbridge onto a walled lane. When the walled lane ends stay with the left wall/fence to join a clear farm track.

16 *(GR 939 764)* Go through the stile and continue to a fork *(SP Footpath)*. Take the right fork and follow the path through a gate. Turn right towards the river and then follow the river upstream over 3 step stiles and a gap stile to reach the road.

17 *(GR 940 773)* Turn right and follow the road over the river bridge. At the village green turn left onto a rough track and climb up to the entrance of the car park.

CAM HEAD and MOOR END FELL

from Kettlewell (6¼ miles)

Starting from the lovely village of Kettlewell, this moderate hill walk follows former packhorse and drovers' roads. There are some excellent views of the valley on both outward and return journeys.

Kettlewell is situated at the foot of Great Whernside which, at 2312 feet, is Wharfedale's highest mountain. The scenery and contour of the mountains around Kettlewell are said to be a near facsimile of the Valley of Jehoshaphat in Palestine.

The village was granted a market charter in 1320 and became a thriving centre for the dale. At one time it had five inns, a beerhouse, a cotton mill, three schools, three blacksmiths and a surgeon.

The manor of Kettlewell was once owned by Richard Neville, Earl of Warwick, known as 'the Kingmaker.' After his death at the Battle of Barnet in 1471, his estates were confiscated by the Crown for supporting the enemies of Edward IV. In 1656, the manor was bought by eight trustees for the freeholders of Kettlewell who came to be known as the 'Trust Lords.'

In recent years Kettlewell has been inundated by the arrival of some very strange residents! During the first few weeks of August the village holds its annual scarecrow festival, with almost every household in the community taking part. Hundreds of 'scarecrow residents' are dotted about the village in a wide variety of poses and disguises including burglars, musicians, fishermen and joggers. A few years ago, some visitors were shocked when one scarecrow, with a 'real life resident' hiding inside, spoke to them!

Leaving the village a former packhorse route, the Top Mere Road, leads to Cam Head. During the ascent views extend to Kilnsey Crag and its striking overhang.

This ancient track passes the site of the chimney and flue which served the Kettlewell Smelt Mill. The mill started work towards the end of the seventeenth century. It was rebuilt in 1868 when a long flue was constructed to a high chimney on the side of Cam Pasture. The mill closed in 1887 and was in good condition until it was demolished by the army in 1942 to test a new type of explosive. However, the chimney had blown down during a gale in 1893.

At Cam Head the route joins the Starbotton Road. This is an old drovers' track which linked Coverdale and Malhamdale. During the descent to Starbotton there are sweeping views across the valley of Old Cote Moor and Moor End Fell.

Although sited on a busy main road, Starbotton has retained a peaceful outlook. The name is of Norse origin meaning 'the valley where the stakes were cut.' Many of the buildings in the village were rebuilt after the disastrous flood of 1686. The Fox and Hounds Inn, which was rebuilt in 1834, is a welcome oasis for weary travellers.

After crossing the River Wharfe the path climbs steeply through a wood and emerges onto the shoulder of Moor End Fell. From here the steep sides and U-shaped valley floor, which are typical of glacial action, can be seen to best advantage.

Moor End Farm, which is now an Outward Bound Centre, was built for the manager of the nearby leadmines in the early eighteenth century. The Moor End mines were heavily worked between 1731 and 1879. A shaft was sunk to a depth of 210 feet and one level was worked for 2000 feet. Most of the ore was sent to the Cupola Smelt Mill at Starbotton.

From Moor End the path descends gently on its return to Kettlewell. Across the river, on the lower slopes, lynchets are visible when the sun is low.

Start/Parking:	Kettlewell YDNP car park.
Location:	Kettlewell is situated on the B6160 14 miles north of Skipton.
Grid Ref:	968 723.
Distance:	6¼ miles circular. Allow 3¾ hrs.
OS Maps:	Outdoor Leisure Map 30 (1:25,000) or Landranger 98 (1:50,000).
Refreshments:	The Bluebell Hotel, The Racehorses, The King's Head and several tea rooms at Kettlewell. The Fox and Hounds at Starbotton.
Public Toilets:	Kettlewell near the bridge at the centre of the village.
Other:	Post office, telephone, limited bus service, shops.

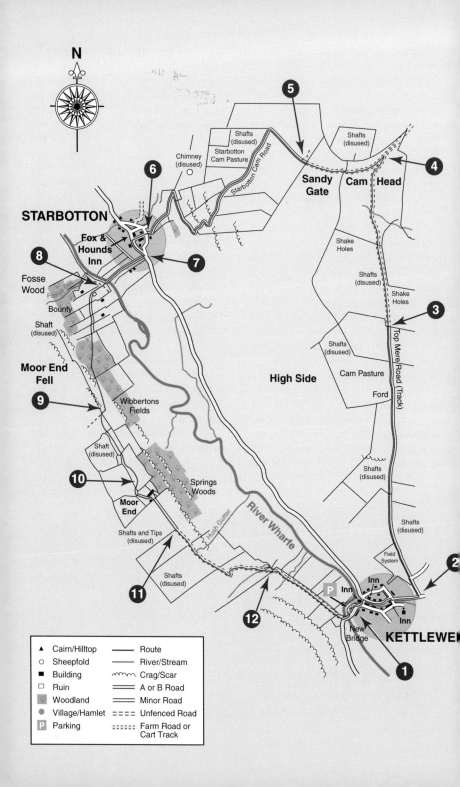

8 Cam Head and Moor End Fell

1 *(GR 968 723)* From the car park turn left and follow the road over the river bridge. Turn right immediately and continue to the junction by the Post Office. Cross the junction and take the Leyburn road out of the village.

2 *(GR 973 724)* Turn left and follow the road uphill. At the next bend leave the road to join an enclosed stone track *(SP Bridleway Starbotton)*. Begin the steep ascent to Cam Head passing through two gated stiles.

3 *(GR 971 742)* From this stile the track becomes unenclosed, continue climbing and go through another gate. Stay on the track to a cairn/signpost.

4 *(GR 971 753)* Turn left at the cairn onto a clear track *(SP Starbotton)*. From this point the track levels out traversing the hillside. At the next gate the track descends through Sandy Gate pasture.

5 *(GR 965 753)* Go through the gate to join the Starbotton Cam Road. This enclosed track leads all the way down to Starbotton via only two gates.

6 *(GR 954 748)* Cross to the lane opposite and follow it to the main road. Turn left and continue on the road towards Kettlewell.

7 *(GR 954 747)* Turn right onto a walled track *(SP Arncliffe/Kettlewell/Buckden)*. Cross the river bridge and go through a gate.

8 *(GR 951 745)* Continue straight ahead *(SP Arncliffe)*, follow a tree lined path between broken walls to a ruined barn. Bear left and begin a steady climb, keeping to the wall side. Cross several broken walls and go through a gate. Continue climbing through a small wood. Leave the wood via a gate at the top and follow the path to reach a gate.

9 *(GR 951 736)* Go through the gate and bear left *(SP Kettlewell)*. Continue through two gates towards Moor End Farm.

10 *(GR 954 732)* Bear right *(SP Bridleway)* and climb to go through the gate in the corner of the right wall. Follow the left wall round and go through another gate. Keep close to the left wall and pass in front of the farmhouse. Turn right and go through a gate to the left of a barn. Stay with the left wall and continue on a broad path to an open gateway.

11 *(GR 956 728)* From this point the path changes into a rough farm track. Stay on the track and descend steadily through the next two pastures and then descend steeply to the wall at the bottom left of the field.

12 *(GR 962 726)* Go through three gates and onto the main road near New Bridge. Turn left and follow the road over the bridge returning to the car park.

Starbotton and Cam Gill

HUBBERHOLME, YOCKENTHWAITE & CRAY

from Buckden (6¾ miles)

The rich and varied landscape of Langstrothdale is explored during this leisurely walk. The outward route follows the riverside and the high level return has fine views of the valley and surrounding fells.

At Buckden the main valley bears left and follows the River Wharfe upstream towards its source on Cam Fell. This unspoiled valley is known as Langstrothdale which means 'the valley of the long stretch of marsh overgrown with brushwood.' It was a feudal hunting forest which belonged to the mighty Percy family and had ten hunting lodges. Langstrothdale was described by Chaucer, in his *Reeve's Tale,* as "farre in the north can I not tell where."

Leaving Buckden the route follows the Dales Way along the valley bottom to the hamlet of Hubberholme.

Hubberholme was first named Huburgheham, meaning 'Hunberg's enclosure,' and is one of the few places named after a woman. The George Inn was Hubberholme's vicarage until 1893 and it maintains a 200 year old land letting ceremony. Every New Year's Day a 'candle auction' is held for the letting of a field behind the inn. At the start of the auction a candle is lit and the final bid has to be made before it burns out. The serious bidding takes place when the candle begins to flicker. The proceeds from the auction are used to help the old people of the parish.

Across the bridge is the impressive church of St. Michael and All Angels, which was originally a forest chapel known as St. Oswald's and later St. Leonard's. The main building work was completed in the twelfth century. It has a finely carved oak rood loft, painted red, gold and black, erected in 1558. In the twentieth century Robert Thompson, the 'Mouseman' of Kilburn, carved the pews which bear his famous trademark. A plaque acknowledges that J. B. Priestley, the playwright, is interred in the churchyard. He longed to run the George Inn and considered Hubberholme to be "the most peaceful spot on earth."

Continuing along the Dales Way to Yockenthwaite, a wide variety of birds may be seen. These include wheatears, dippers, meadow pipits, grey wagtails and kingfishers.

Yockenthwaite, or 'Yokanwit' as it is known locally, is of Irish-Norse origin and means 'Eoghan's clearing.' In 1241, it was called Yoghannesthweit and the parish register of 1745 shows it as 'Yoke and White.' The hamlet is situated on a former packhorse route linking Ribblesdale with Wensleydale. It has a delightful single arched stone bridge shaded by sycamores.

After a gentle climb from Yockenthwaite a level limestone terrace is followed to Scar House.

George Fox, the founder of the Society of Friends or 'Quakers,' visited Scar House in 1652. He stayed with James Tennant and his family, who were converted to the 'new religion.' Scar House became a regular meeting house. James Tennant died at York Castle, where he had been imprisoned for his beliefs. He was buried in the Quaker burial ground at Scar House, which became the property of the Society of Friends in 1709.

The route continues on an almost level track above wooded limestone scars with good views of Buckden Pike, Birks Fell, Langstrothdale and Upper Wharfedale.

Although it was once a much larger settlement, the tiny hamlet of Cray now consists of a few farm buildings and the White Lion Inn, The village takes its name from the Celtic 'crei' which means 'the fresh stream.' If time allows, a short detour should be made to visit the striking waterfall at Cray Gill.

From Cray an easy climb leads to Buckden Rake which is followed back to the car park at Buckden.

Start/Parking:	Buckden YDNP car park.
Location:	Buckden is situated on the B6160 4 miles north of Kettlewell and 18 miles north of Skipton.
Grid Ref:	942 773.
Distance:	6¾ miles circular. Allow 3¼ hrs.
OS Maps:	Outdoor Leisure Map 30 (1:25,000) or Landranger 98 (1:50,000).
Refreshments:	The Buck Inn and The Village Tea Rooms at Buckden, The George Inn at Hubberholme, The White Lion Inn at Cray.
Public Toilets:	Buckden near the entrance to the car park.
Other:	Post office, telephone, limited bus service, shops.

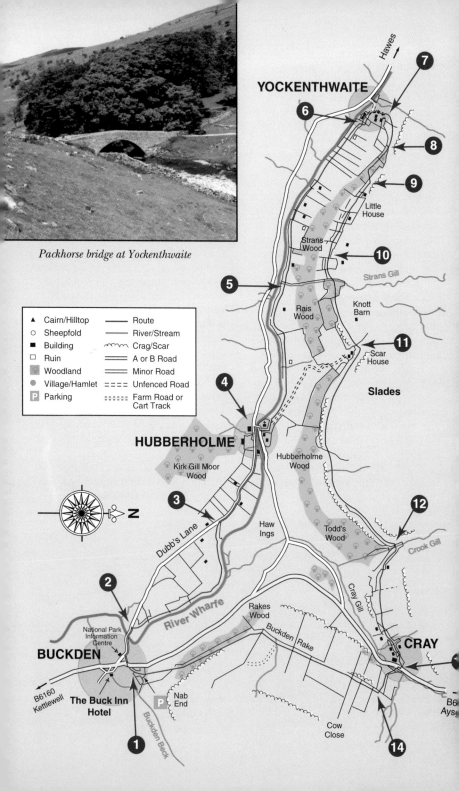

Packhorse bridge at Yockenthwaite

YOCKENTHWAITE

Hawes

Little House

Strans Wood

Strans Gill

Rais Wood

Knott Barn

Scar House

Slades

HUBBERHOLME

Kirk Gill Moor Wood

Hubberholme Wood

Dubb's Lane

Haw Ings

Todd's Wood

Crook Gill

National Park Information Centre

BUCKDEN

River Wharfe

Rakes Wood

Buckden Rake

Cray Gill

CRAY

B6160 Kettlewell

The Buck Inn Hotel

P

Nab End

Buckden Beck

Cow Close

B6 Ays

▲ Cairn/Hilltop	▬▬ Route
○ Sheepfold	▬▬ River/Stream
■ Building	∿∿∿ Crag/Scar
□ Ruin	▬▬ A or B Road
Woodland	▬▬ Minor Road
● Village/Hamlet	==== Unfenced Road
P Parking	⋯⋯ Farm Road or Cart Track

N

9 Hubberholme, Yockenthwaite and Cray

1 *(GR 942 773)* Leave the car park by the entrance. Turn left, after a few yards cross the road and turn right onto a rough track. Follow this track down to the Hubberholme road. Turn right and continue on the road to cross the river bridge.

2 *(GR 940 773)* Leave the road over a stile *(SP Hubberholme)*. Bear left and follow the riverside over 3 wooden step stiles and through a gate returning to the road.

3 *(GR 932 780)* Turn right and follow the road to the George Inn at Hubberholme.

4 *(GR 926 782)* Turn right at the George Inn and cross the bridge. After a few yards leave the road through a gate which leads behind Hubberholme Church *(SP Scar House/Yockenthwaite)*. At the back of the church take the left path *(SP Yockenthwaite/ Dales Way)*. Continue on a clear path along the riverside to Strans Gill.

5 *(GR 917 784)* Cross the footbridge/stile combination. Follow the path through two stiles, where the path becomes enclosed between the river and the wall. Pass through a gate and a gap stile before returning to the open fields. Continue through several meadows to reach Yockenthwaite.

6 *(GR 906 790)* Bear right and go through a gap stile, then bear left and go through two gates to enter the hamlet. Follow the farm road towards Yockenthwaite bridge, **BUT** turn sharp right at a fork onto another farm track which climbs up to the left of the farmhouse. Follow the farm track behind the tree *(SP Cray/Hubberholme)*.

7 *(GR 905 791)* When the farm track bears right towards the back of a cottage leave it and climb up to a rough stone track *(SP Cray/Hubberholme)*. Turn right and follow the track uphill.

8 *(GR 908 792)* Leave the track through a gate on the right *(SP)* and follow a stony path through the wood. Go through a gate and follow the path to a footpath sign bear left and climb steeply through the trees to the plateau.

9 *(GR 910 790)* Turn right and continue on a level path through a gate and several broken walls.

10 *(GR 915 787)* Go through two gap stiles, bear left at the fence and climb slightly to cross Strans Gill over a footbridge to enter a wood. Continue through the wood, cross a stile to join a clear path which leads through a gap stile to Scar House.

11 *(GR 921 789)* From the stile bear right towards the farmhouse and after a few yards climb up the outcrop to the left of the wood *(SP Cray)*. Follow a clear path above the trees staying close to the wall side to reach Crook Gill.

12 *(GR 934 792)* Cross Crook Gill over a footbridge, turn right and climb to a barn. Go through the gate next to the barn and continue through the pastures to join a stone track which leads into Cray emerging onto the road by the White Lion Inn.

13 *(GR 942 792)* Cross the road and then cross Cray Gill at the stepping stones. Bear right and go through a gate *(SP Cray Bridge/Buckden)*. Follow the path uphill and go through a gate in the centre of the top wall.

14 *(GR 944 791)* Turn right and go through a stile. Continue on a level path through four pastures. Here the track gets rougher and after going through the next gate it descends steeply down through Rakes Wood, returning to the car park.

YOCKENTHWAITE and BECKERMONDS

from Halton Gill (8 miles)

Wild moorland and riverside paths provide contrasts of scenery throughout this demanding hill walk. It crosses into Langstrothdale and visits the head of the River Wharfe.

Halton Gill is a peaceful hamlet occupying a picturesque setting at the foot of Horse Head Moor. Most of the buildings date from the seventeenth century. The Hall, built in 1641, has fine mullioned windows and a two-storey porch. The former church and schoolhouse bear the date 1626 and WF, the initials of William Fawcett a wealthy Norwich wool merchant, who settled here after the Dissolution.

Here the Rev. Miles Wilson, curate of Halton Gill from 1737 to 1776,

wrote 'The Man in the Moon.' The story relates to the adventures of Israel Jobson, a cobbler from Horton-in-Ribblesdale. He erected a ladder on top of Penyghent and climbed to the Moon. He soon returned because he was dissatisfied with the food!

The path to Yockenthwaite follows the old packhorse route from Settle to Hawes. Until the end of the nineteenth century packhorses were the main form of transport. Horses and ponies carried up to two hundred-weight of merchandise divided into two panniers or baskets. Packhorse trains consisted of up to forty animals carrying coal, cereals, salt, meat, and wool. They were usually escorted by a driver and one or two assistants.

The ordnance survey column on the summit of Horse Head Moor commands one of the finest viewpoints in the dales. Fountains Fell, Penyghent, Ingleborough and Whernside compete with views of Langdale Pike, Wild Boar Fell and Great Shunner Fell. Completing the panorama are the tops of Penhill, Buckden Pike and Great Whernside to the east.

From Horse Head Gate the route descends steeply to Yockenthwaite. Yockenthwaite occupies a beautiful position above the River Wharfe. It is linked to the road by a charming single arched packhorse bridge. At one time the hamlet had sixteen houses, an inn and a school. Its decline began in the nineteenth century with the introduction of the turnpike roads and the railways. By the 1851 census it was reduced to only four houses.

Upstream from the village there is a Bronze Age stone circle known as the Giant's Grave. The circle measures twenty five feet across and consists of twenty stones. There are signs that it may also have had an outer circle. From its location it is more likely to have been a burial mound rather than a place of worship.

Deepdale is another hamlet which has dwindled in size. Langstrothdale once carried the main coaching road from Lancaster to Newcastle-upon-Tyne and at that time Deepdale was an important staging post. It had thirteen houses, two inns and a smithy. Today, only two houses remain. The coaches entered the dale near Greenfield and followed the course of the River Wharfe to Hubberholme, continuing via Cray and the Kidstones Pass into Wensleydale.

The route from Deepdale follows a leisurely stretch of the River Wharfe to Beckermonds, whose name means 'the meeting of the streams.' Here the waters of Greenfield Beck converge with Oughtershaw Beck giving birth to the River Wharfe. Dippers can be seen throughout the year along this stretch of the River and pied wagtails, grey wagtails and kingfishers frequent it during the summer months.

From Beckermonds a steep path climbs to the summit of Eller Scar and returns into Littondale. Watch out for peregrine falcons which have been spotted in this area. The descent to Halton Gill provides fine views of Foxup and Cosh at the upper reaches of Littondale.

Start/Parking:	Halton Gill, limited parking.
Location:	Halton Gill is located 19 miles north of Skipton. Leave the B6160 after passing Kilnsey signposted Arncliffe 3 miles.
Grid Ref:	881 765.
Distance:	8 miles circular. Allow 4 hrs.
OS Maps:	Outdoor Leisure Map 30 (1:25,000) or Landranger 98 (1:50,000).
Refreshments:	None.
Public Toilets:	None.
Other:	Telephone.

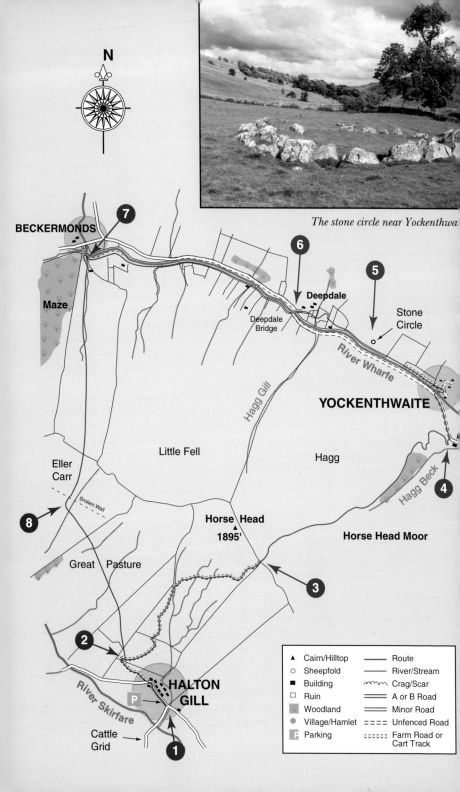

N

BECKERMONDS

Maze

7

6 **Deepdale**

Deepdale
Bridge

5 Stone
Circle

The stone circle near Yockenthwa

River Wharfe

YOCKENTHWAITE

Hagg Gill

Little Fell

Eller
Carr

Broken Wall

8

Hagg

Hagg Beck

4

Horse Head
1895'

Horse Head Moor

Great Pasture

3

2

River Skirfare

P

**HALTON
GILL**

Cattle
Grid

1

Symbol	Legend	Symbol	Legend
▲	Cairn/Hilltop		Route
○	Sheepfold		River/Stream
■	Building	∿∿∿	Crag/Scar
□	Ruin		A or B Road
	Woodland		Minor Road
	Village/Hamlet	= = =	Unfenced Road
P	Parking	⋯⋯⋯	Farm Road or Cart Track

10 Horse Head Moor and Beckermonds

1 *(GR 881 765)* Take the Foxup road out of the village and at the last building on the left leave the road through a gate on the right *(SP Beckermonds/Yockenthwaite)*. Follow a broad track uphill and go through a gate.

2 *(GR 877 768)* From the gate continue ahead on the broad track *(SP Route to Yockenthwaite)*.Climb through two gates to Horse Head Gate.

3 *(GR 889 776)* Continue straight ahead to cross the summit and then begin the steady descent to the road near the cattle grid just outside Yockenthwaite.

4 *(GR 906 706)* Turn left and follow the road to the packhorse bridge. Cross the bridge and follow the farm road to the left to reach a signpost behind a tree. Turn left *(SP Beckermonds/Deepdale/Dalesway)* and follow a rough track through a gate. Continue through two pastures to Yockenthwaite stone circle.

5 *(GR 899 794)* From the circle continue through an open gateway and over two ladder stiles. Follow the signs and cross a wooden bridge, a clear track leads through a gate on to the farm road at Deepdale. Turn left and continue down to the main road.

6 *(GR 892 797)* Turn left and cross the river bridge. Turn right *(SP Beckermonds)* and follow the river upstream. Cross a ladder stile and continue to a gate.

7 *(GR 874 802)* Go through the gate, follow the right wall to a signpost. Turn left *(SP Halton Gill)* and follow a narrow path uphill. The path is marked with cairns here and there. At the summit cross a ladder stile and continue straight ahead before descending through a broken wall to a markerpost.

8 *(GR 872 781)* Turn left at the marker post and follow a clear path keeping roughly to the same height over two ladder stiles. From the ladder stile descend steeply to a gate in the bottom right corner. Go through the gate and continue along a clear path to reach the gate at point 2. Follow the outward route back to Halton Gill.

Yockenthwaite

BUCKDEN PIKE and THE MEMORIAL CROSS

from Buckden (8 miles)

This is a spectacular walk taking in the summit of Wharfedale's second highest fell. There is a variety of terrain and scenery throughout the walk. The outstanding views instill a feeling of tranquillity.

Buckden is a picturesque village situated at the head of the dale. It was founded during the twelfth century as the headquarters to the foresters of Langstrothdale Chase. The village was named after the deer which roamed in the forest and means 'the valley of the bucks.' Until 1947, there was a herd of fallow deer roaming in the woods across the river. At the centre of the village is the eighteenth century Buck Inn, a traditional coaching inn with great charm and character. The court-

yard, now a restaurant, was once used for local wool auctions.

The early part of the walk climbs through Rakes Wood and follows the course of the Roman road known as Buckden Rake. This was constructed in the first century AD under Roman governor Julius Agricola during his campaigns to subdue the Celtic tribes of Yorkshire. It provided a vital link between the forts at Ilkley *(Olicana)* and Bainbridge *(Virosidum)*. At the end of the wood there are views of Wharfedale, Hubberholme Church and Langstrothdale.

From the windswept heights of Buckden Pike, which stands at 2302 feet, views extend in every direction. Great Whernside lies to the south,

Penyghent, Ingleborough and Fountains Fell lie to the west. To the east, on a clear day, York Minster can be seen.

In 1880, the Skipton and Kettlewell Railway Company made proposals to tunnel under Buckden Pike. Its intention was to extend the line from Skipton to Buckden and on to link with the North Eastern Railway near Aysgarth Station in Wensleydale. This would have involved the construction of a 2410 yard tunnel into Wensleydale. The proposals also required the building of a bridge to span the river at Aysgarth Falls. This led to an outcry across the country. Alternative routes were suggested, but they had to be abandoned due to lack of capital.

The path beside the summit wall leads to the memorial cross. In 1942, an RAF Wellington bomber with a crew of six Polish airmen crashed near this site during a blizzard. There was one survivor. He suffered a broken leg, but managed to crawl out from the wreckage. He came across the tracks of a fox in the snow. Considering that foxes usually hunt for food close to human dwellings, he decided to take a chance and followed the tracks. He dragged himself downhill through the snow eventually reaching the safety of a farm near Cray.

To give thanks for his deliverance and in memory of his five comrades he had the cross erected on this site. In recognition of the fox's part in the story he set a bronze fox's head into the foundation along with fragments from the wreckage.

From the memorial the route descends to join the Walden Road, a former packhorse trail which links Wharfedale to Wensleydale. The views of the valley and surrounding fells are enjoyed all the way to Starbotton.

Starbotton is a peaceful village situated close to the foot of Cam Gill Beck. In 1686, during a terrible storm, the waters of the beck became a raging flood and the village was almost totally destroyed. Many cottages were washed away and those that survived were filled with mud and stones up to the first floor. The debris covered acres of meadowland and the damage was estimated at £3000. A national appeal raised money from all over England to help with the rebuilding of the village.

The return to Buckden follows a section of the Dales Way footpath and provides a delightful finish to the walk. There are many species of birds to be seen here including dippers, sandpipers, herons and, with luck, kingfishers.

Start/Parking:	Buckden YDNP car park.
Location:	Buckden is situated on the B6160 4 miles north of Kettlewell and 18 miles north of Skipton.
Grid Ref:	942 773.
Distance:	8 miles circular. Allow $4\frac{1}{2}$ hrs.
OS Maps:	Outdoor Leisure Map 30 (1:25,000) or Landranger 98 (1:50,000).
Refreshments:	The Buck Inn and The Village Tea Rooms at Buckden, The Fox & Hounds at Starbotton.
Public Toilets:	Buckden near the entrance to the YDNP car park.
Other:	Post office, telephone, limited bus service, shops.

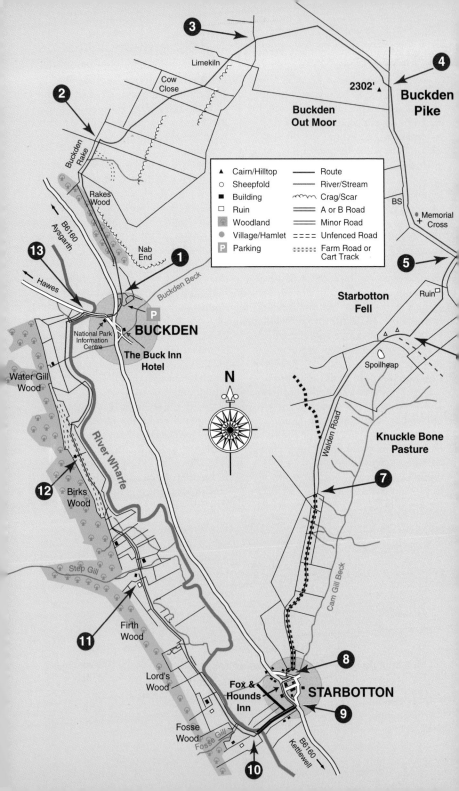

11   Buckden Pike and The Memorial Cross

1 *(GR 942 773)* Leave the car park by a gate at the northern end *(SP Buckden Pike)*. Follow a stony track which climbs gently up through Rakes Wood. At the end of the wood the track bears right and passes through a gate where the track levels out. Continue by the wall to the next gate.

2 *(GR 941 784)* Go through the gate and bear right *(SP Buckden Pike)*. The path soon becomes clearer, climbing diagonally across the field to another gate. Go through this gate and continue uphill crossing 4 more pastures to reach another gate.

3 *(GR 952 791)* Go through the gate onto the open moor *(SP Buckden Pike)* and climb up through a small gully. At the top of the gully the path meanders uphill towards the left wall. On reaching the wall by a footpath sign climb up alongside it to the summit.

4 *(GR 961 789)* Cross the ladder stile, turn right and follow the wall to the Memorial Cross. From the memorial continue with the wall and descend to a boundary gate on the right. *(See note at foot of page)*

5 *(GR 966 777)* Go through the gate and join a level track, this is the Walden Road. After going through the next wall the track begins a steep descent.

6 *(GR 962 771)* Bear right and follow the cairns, go through a gateway to join a clearer track. This track leads through another gateway and descends alongside the left wall.

7 *(GR 956 761)* Go through the gateway, from here the track is clear and leads all the way down to Starbotton.

8 *(GR 953 749)* Turn left, cross the bridge and turn right. Continue along this lane to reach the main road by the Fox and Hounds Inn. Turn left and follow the road towards Kettlewell.

9 *(GR 954 747)* Turn right onto a walled track *(SP Arncliffe/Kettlewell/Buckden)*. Cross the river bridge and go through the gate.

10 *(GR 951 745)* Turn right *(SP Buckden)* and follow the river upstream. Cross a small footbridge and continue over 2 stiles. At this point the path leaves the river and stays close to the left wall.

11 *(GR 944 755)* Cross a ladder stile by a ruined barn, continue through a gate and over a footbridge onto a walled lane. When the walled lane ends stay with the left wall/fence to join a clear farm track.

12 *(GR 939 764)* Go through the stile and continue to a fork *(SP Footpath)*. Take the right fork and follow the path through a gate. Turn right towards the river and then follow the river upstream over 3 step stiles and a gap stile to reach the road.

13 *(GR 940 773)* Turn right and follow the road over the river bridge. At the village green turn left onto a rough track and climb up to the entrance of the car park.

IMPORTANT NOTE

At the time of going to press the route between point 4 and point 5 was not a public right of way, although it has been used regularly by walkers for many years without any problems. Discussions between the landowners and the National Park Authority were taking place to obtain permission to use the route as a permissive path. Its inclusion is not, for legal reasons, claimed as evidence of any right of way.

Information Desk

ABBEYS

Bolton Priory, Bolton Abbey
A twelfth century Augustinian Priory, the nave now serves as the parish church of St Mary and St. Cuthbert. Open daily from 8.30am to 7pm *(or dusk if earlier).* Closes 4pm on Fridays. Guides are available for groups by prior arrangement. (01756) 710238.

CASTLES

Skipton Castle, Skipton
One of the best preserved mediaeval castles in England still fully roofed. It was besieged by Oliver Cromwell. Monday to Saturday 10am, Sunday 12 noon. Last admission March to September 6pm, October to February 4pm. Closed Christmas Day. (01756) 792442.

CRAFT CENTRES

Acorns to Oak, Main Street, Grassington
Traditional furniture.
(01756) 753045.

CYCLE HIRE

Dave Ferguson Cycles,
1 Brook Street, Skipton (01756) 795367.

Dalesman Cafe,
54 High Street, Gargrave (01756) 749250.

Kettlewell Garage, Kettlewell
(01756) 760225.

GARDENS

Parcevall Hall, Skyreholme, Appletreewick
Sixteen acres of beautiful woodland gardens, rock gardens and terraces. Home to choice trees, shrubs, bulbs and herbaceous plants.
Easter to end October 10.00am to 6.00pm. (1756) 720311

HISTORIC HOUSES

Barden Tower, Bolton Abbey
An eleventh century hunting lodge, rebuilt and enlarged in 1485 and refurbished in the seventeenth century by Lady Anne Clifford.
Open daily.

Broughton Hall, nr Skipton
Open Bank Holiday Mondays 11am to 4pm. Tours every hour on the hour. (01756) 799608.

LEISURE PARKS

Coniston Hall Estate, Coniston Cold, nr Skipton
Fishing, shooting, leisure and tea room.
Open daily from 10am. (01756) 748136.

Kilnsey Park, Kilnsey
Dales life centre, trout viewing and feeding areas, fly fishing, nature trail, restaurant and cafe.
Daily 9am to 5.30pm *(or dusk in winter).* (01756) 752150.

MUSEUMS

The Craven Museum, High Street, Skipton
April to September: Sunday 2pm to 5pm, Monday to Friday (not Tuesday) 10am to 5pm, Saturday 10am to 12 noon and 1pm to 5pm. *October to March:* Monday to Friday (not Tuesday) 10am to 5pm, Saturday 10am to 12 noon and 1pm to 4pm, Closed Sundays. Check for Bank Holidays. (01756) 706407.

The Manor House Museum and Art Gallery
Castle Yard, Ilkley
The museum is built on the site of the Roman Fort of Olicana. It has a number of Roman exhibits found locally and some fine tombstones. The gallery promotes the work of local artists.
Wednesday to Saturday 11am to 5pm, Sunday 1pm to 4pm. Open Bank Holiday Monday. (01943) 600066.

Upper Wharfedale Museum,
The Square, Grassington
Exhibits of lead mining, minerals, craft tools, lathes, Dales farming, period costumes, folk lore etc.
Open daily April 1st to End September 2pm to 4.30pm. Winter: Saturday and Sunday only. Other times by arrangement. (01756) 753059.

OUTDOOR CENTRES

Buckden House, Buckden
Abseiling, adventure trails, archery, canoeing, caving, climbing, cycling, fell walking, orienteering.
(01756) 760254.

RIDING & PONY TREKKING

Draughton Heights Riding Stables, Draughton
(01756) 710242.

Kilnsey Trekking Centre, Conistone, Grassington
(01756) 752861.

SHOW CAVES

Stump Cross Caverns, Grassington/Pateley Bridge
The underground wonders are easily reached via steps and gravel paths.
Open Daily Easter to October 10am onwards. Winter: Saturday and Sunday 11am to 4pm. School parties by appointment throughout the year. Check in winter during poor weather. (01756) 752780 or (01423) 711282.

STEAM TRAINS

Embsay Steam Railway, Embsay, nr Skipton
Steam trains every Sunday throughout the year and up to 5 days a week in Summer.
(01756) 794727. Talking Timetable (01756) 795189.

SWIMMING POOLS

Skipton, Gargrave Road
(01756) 792805.

Threshfield, Long Ashes
(01756) 753520.

TOURIST INFORMATION POINTS

Bolton Abbey, The Cavendish Pavilion.

Buckden, The Riverside Gallery.

Burnsall, The Post Office.

Grassington, The National Park Centre.

Hebden, The Post Office.

Kettlewell, Over and Under outdoor shop.

Kilnsey, Kilnsey Park Aquarium.

Litton, The Post Office.

The Country Code

Enjoy the countryside and respect its life and works

Keep to public paths across farmland

Leave livestock, crops and farm machinery alone

Use gates and stiles to cross fences, hedges and walls

Guard against all risks of fire

Make no unnecessary noise

Fasten all gates

Take your litter home

Help to keep all water clean

Protect wildlife, plants and trees

Take special care on country roads

Keep your dogs under close control

Also . . .

Use car parks where possible and park with consideration for village residents and other road users.

Don't obstruct farm gates, tracks or entrances.

When walking on roads, walk on the right hand side to face oncoming traffic. When approaching blind bends, cross to the opposite side to enable you to see and be seen in both directions.

Allow sufficient time to complete the walk in daylight hours, and be sure to be off the fells by dusk.

Let people know the route you have taken, the time you expect to return and stick to the route.

If the weather turns nasty and you decide to quit the walk or take shelter in a hostelry etc, be sure to let others know so they don't worry and call out the emergency services unnecessarily.

Glossary

Most of the place names in Wharfedale are Anglo-Saxon or Norse in origin. Anglo-Saxon names include those ending with *ing, ley, ham* and *ton*. Norse names include those ending with *by, sett* and *thwaite*. The Normans had a smaller influence on place names, being confined to changes in the spelling of existing names. They gave us the Domesday Book in 1086 recording the name, population and value of each village.

Appletreewick:	The dairy farm by the apple tree
Arncliffe:	The eagles' cliff
Arncliffe Cote:	The cottage belonging to Arncliffe.
Barden:	The barley valley.
Beck:	Stream.
Beckermonds:	The meeting place of the streams.
Blubberhouses:	The houses by the spring.
Buckden:	The valley of the bucks..
Burnsall:	Bryni's nook of land.
Calgarth:	The kitchen garden.
Capplestone:	The stony place where horses gather.
Clowder:	The mass of rocks.
Conistone:	The king's farm.
Cosh:	The hovel in the green field.
Cracoe:	Crow Hill.
Craven:	The place where garlic grows.
Cray:	The fresh stream.
Dibb, River:	The pool.
Dibble's Bridge:	The bridge over the pool.
Drebley:	Drebba's clearing.
Elbolton:	The village among the alder trees.
Eller Beck:	The alder stream.
Foss(e):	Waterfall.
Foxup:	The fox valley.
Garnshaw:	The demon's wood.
Gate-up:	The valley with a road.
Ghaistrill's Strid:	Ghaistrill's striding place.
Gill, Ghyll:	A deep wooded ravine.
Grassington:	The farm among the pastures.
Grimwith:	The goblin's wood.
Halton Gill:	Farm in a nook by the ravine.
Hartlington:	Heortla's farm.
Hawkswick:	Hauk's dairy farm.
Hazelwood:	The hazel wood.
Hebden:	The bramble valley.

Hesleden:	The hazel valley.
Howgill:	The hollow ravine.
Hubberholme:	Hunberg's enclosure.
Kail Hill:	The hill with the cabbages growing.
Kettlewell:	The bubbling spring.
Kidstones:	The kid-goat stones.
Kilnsey:	The marsh near the kiln.
Kirk Gill:	The ravine by the church.
Knipe:	The rocky scar.
Knott:	A rocky hill-top.
Lainger:	A place to stay or linger.
Langstrothdale:	The valley of the long stretch of marsh overgrown with brushwood.
Linton:	The flax farm.
Litton:	The farm on the slope.
Littondale:	The valley of Litton.
Old Cote:	Cottages frequented by owls.
Oughtershaw:	Uthred's copse.
Poshforth Gill:	The ravine at Posi's ford.
Raisgill:	The ravine with a cairn.
Rake:	Sheep or cattle path.
Rylestone:	Brook farm.
Skirfare, River:	The bright river.
Skyreholme:	The bright water meadow.
Skythorns:	The bright thorns.
Stake Pass:	The pass marked by stakes.
Starbotton:	The valley where the stakes were cut.
Storiths:	The plantations.
Strid, The:	The striding place.
Swinden:	The swine valley.
Thorpe:	The outlying farmstead.
Threapland:	The disputed land.
Threshfield:	The threshing field.
Troller's Gill:	The troll's arse ravine.
Wharfe, River:	The winding river.
Wharfedale:	The valley of the River Wharfe.
Yockenthwaite:	Eoghan's clearing.